MY PHONE LIES TO ME

Before you start to read this book, take this moment to think about making a donation to punctum books, an independent non-profit press,

@ https://punctumbooks.com/support/

If you're reading the e-book, you can click on the image below to go directly to our donations site. Any amount, no matter the size, is appreciated and will help us to keep our ship of fools afloat. Contributions from dedicated readers will also help us to keep our commons open and to cultivate new work that can't find a welcoming port elsewhere. Our adventure is not possible without your support.

Vive la Open Access.

Fig. 1. Detail from Hieronymus Bosch, *Ship of Fools* (1490–1500)

First published in 2022 by punctum books, Earth, Milky Way.
https://punctumbooks.com

ISBN-13: 978-1-68571-068-2 (print)
ISBN-13: 978-1-68571-069-9 (ePDF)

DOI: 10.53288/0394.1.00

LCCN: 2022948536
Library of Congress Cataloging Data is available from the Library of Congress

Book design: Vincent W.J. van Gerven Oei
Cover design: Cynthia Madansky

HIC SVNT MONSTRA

MY

Fake News Poetry Workshops

PHONE

As Radical Digital Media Literacy

LIES

Given the Fact of Fake News

TO ME

Poems created at 20+ Fake News Poetry Workshops, 2018–20,
in the US, England, the Netherlands, and Canada

In conversation with people, poems, social media, and
the #100hardtruths–#fakenews primer on digital media literacy

With short essays by Alexandra Juhasz, project organizer
A foreword by Tara McPherson
And an afterword by Margaret Rhee

p.

Table of Contents

Acknowledgments

I believe in processes and people. In this effort, poems are made from them. These poems, and associated writings collected here, were written to "teach and tell, count and swell" about some truths about contemporary internet culture (this is also the title of the #100th #hardtruths of my 2017 born-digital primer on digital media literacy, #100hardtruths–#fakenews, which was the first of many iterations of this project in radical digital media literacy).

I thank the many diverse poets whose work is collected here (and elsewhere, online and off, please see the Precis of Process and Participants & Supporters), for their wisdom and willingness to engage and share. I extend that forward. This project is foremost an invitation and invocation for you to join us and participate in an experiment in knowing and working with the internet differently. The radical digital media literacy is when you too read, write, and share; on paper, laptop, phone, or face to face; about truth, lies, and the digital.

Poems are neither easy to make nor publish. So, I thank the 100-plus Fake News Poetry Workshop participants, their twenty-plus teacher-collaborators, and the many institutions, friends, and supporters who wrote and underwrote these poems and their workshops and processes. At the beginning of this volume, a Precis offers you a brief schematic of some of these workshops and their places and people, as well as relevant sister iterations of this sprawling, multi-modal, many-year project. I hope that this will orient and situate your reading in the complex network of people, commitments, and technologies that are the radical digital media literacy I cherish. At the end of this volume, please see and celebrate with me a more expanded list of people, institutions, supporters, and project iterations.

Throughout the project, I have used the changing affordances of its technologies to document, share, and honor its many people, places, and outputs. Snapshots, fliers, reflective writings, and poems from all the workshops can be found on the project's digital repository, fakenews-poetry.org. I thank the design team at Partner&Partners for their work on this, one of many beautiful homes, for the project. Given that this is a book of poems by many people from lots of places about the digital, and the project has lived in material and digital formats, I thank Lily Brewer at punctum books for working with me to devise some solutions to the thorny questions of hyper-links, citational practices, and publishing protocols for paper. I also thank the Co-Directors at punctum books, Vincent W.J. van Gerven Oei and Eileen A. Fradenburg Joy, and the community of fellow authors they support, for providing a perfect home for this innovative project at the intersections of academia, civic action, education, the digital, and poetry.

The project's many participants and supporters are members of interlocking communities of thinkers, artists, and activists whose work sustains me, and this effort. I asked busy people to write or read things, so that together we could think, teach, and make art about the serious and complex troubles of fake news. They did. Scores of friends and colleagues authored their own #100hardtruths, read a poem, connected with or thought alongside another's writing, and nourished the effort with their own work and time in a variety of project iterations: the 2017 primer #100hardtruths–#fakenews; Fake News Poetry Workshops commencing in 2018; writing about those workshops in 2018 for the series "Field Notes: Open Source Creative Process Documentation," itself a project of the Operating System & Liminal Labs; and in our 2020 podcast, *We Need Gentle Truths for Now,* an extension of the project built during a summer of Covid-19 lockdown and Black Lives Matter protests. For those sister projects, I thank Craig Dietrich, Xiomara Rodriguez, Adrian Silbernagle, Matthew Hittle, and Julia Gill who engaged in ways at once technical, creative, and supportive.

In this effort, I try to share and encourage radical pedagogic processes. While the poems evince some of this, my prose, and that of the two invited interlocutors for this effort, also attempt to elucidate how and why we might engage differently with social media. I thank scholar–artist–activist Margaret Rhee for her generous agreement to name and place my idiosyncratic project in civic artistic process; and scholar and radical digital publisher, Tara McPherson, for her words that situate this (and earlier efforts) in the space of online activist intellectual expression and our lives as writers and readers. And, as importantly, I acknowledge the steady word control, copywriting, and conceptualizing that helped tame and make more available my prose by the writer, Gavin McCormick. Finally and also at its front, a hats off to the filmmaker and designer, Cynthia Madansky, for the powerful cover.

This project proves that we can gather together in our many local places and use analog structures (about digital things and ways) to generate, hold, and share "art answers to phony questions" (this is one of five overarching adages about fake news that grew from my primer and moved on to do other work for further iterations of the project). Rather than the poetry itself, the process of making poetry (together, in situ, concerning what we know and want to share with others) is the product. Our poems evidence working together about and off the internet as one model for ethical, grounded, careful conversation, interaction, understanding, and communication in our post-truth era.

Precis of Process

Given the many places, homes, technologies, and iterations of this community-based, multi-modal, process-oriented experiment in radical digital media literacy given the fact of fake news, the following precis seeks to situate readers.

Since 2018, project organizer, Alexandra (Alex) Juhasz, has held over 25 Fake News Poetry Workshops around the world, with diverse co-facilitators and poets. Poems selected for this collection were created at some of these workshops. A full and more detailed list of workshops and their participants and supporters can be found at the conclusion of the book. All of the poems written at workshops can be found on the project's repository: fakenews-poetry.org.

Select Fake News Poetry Workshops

Ammerman Center. Sixteenth Biennial Symposium on Arts & Technology. New London, CT. February 15, 2018. Artists and technologists led by poet, technologist, and scholar, Kyle Booten to write poetry algorithms.

ArtEZ University of the Arts. Arnhem, Netherlands. October 17, 2019. Participants included graduate students in Theater Practices with the support of their professors Pavlos Kountouriotis and Nishant Shah and with performance instructions created by Dr. Ioana Jucan.

Brooklyn College. Documentary Across the Disciplines class (DOC@BC). Brooklyn, NY. February 22, 2019. Inter-disciplinary class with professors and students from across the college.

Dartmouth College. Digital Humanities and Social Engagement Center. February 25, 2019. "Algorithms as Pets and Politicians," with Dartmouth students, professors, and staff. Led by Orr Menirom and Kyle Booten who helped us feed bots that spewed some poems.

Devil's Dyke Network. Brighton, England. March 19, 2018. Members, Linda Paoli, Claudia Treacher, and Helen Dixon devised and facilitated a somatic workshop with six others from this queer feminist writing collective to "contest fake/hegemonic media through creative means."

DIGITAL engAGEment: Media. Literate. #activist Conference. Held in Manhattan, NY. May 18, 2018. Workshop led by video artist, Orr Menirom, and attended by conference participants, making use of exquisite corpse production methods.

Feminist Poetics, Emergent Pedagogies Symposium. Los Angeles, CA. May 2018. Elae [Lynne DeSilva-Johnson] led an intimate workshop at the Occidental College Center for Digital Media Arts called Cartographies of Erasure.

HASTAC: Humanities, Arts, Science, and Technology Alliance and Collaboratory Conference. Vancouver, British Columbia. May 18, 2019. And a linked workshop at the **Digital Methods Summer School**. Amsterdam, the Netherlands. The week of July 1, 2019. Both workshops were led by the performance scholar and artist, Dr. Ioana Jucan, in collaboration with digital theorist and artist, Roopa Vasudevan, and used internet memes and project poems as fuel for scripts and performances.

Get Lit. Los Angeles, CA. March 3, 2018. A workshop led by Kelly Grace Thomas with fifteen expert teen poets, Get Lit Players, and a linked video-poetry workshop, October 13, 2018.

Home of T.L. Cowan. Toronto, CA. March 17, 2018. A "a salon of co-creation," led by cabaret-scholar, Dr. Cowan, and attended by media artists, activists, and scholars in town for the Annual Society for Cinema and Media Studies conference.

LaGuardia Community College. Queens, NY. April 24–26, 2018. Led by Lisa Cohen and engaging with scores of students in a poetry workshop, a literary club, and an English 101 class.

New Utrecht High School. Brooklyn, NY. May 7 and 9, 2019. Participants from an after-school arts program run by the Brooklyn College Community Partnership.

New York University. Performative Writing class. April 10, 2019. Undergraduate students in the Performance Studies Department. Co-facilitated by Dr. Barbara Browning.

Poets of Course. Manhattan, NY. October 2, 2018 and throughout Spring 2019. Cathy James working with fifteen or more activated disabled poets in a theater and performance group with countless poems, video-poems, and performances as outcome.

Race in the Media. Brooklyn, NY. May 5, 2018, Led by Chet'la Sebree and Margaret Rhee working with primarily queer poets of color. And a linked video-poem workshop at the **Home of Claudia Rankine and John Lucas.** New Haven, CT. November 3, 2018.

University of Sussex. Falmer, England. March 19 and 20, 2018. Experimental Writing class. Students led by their teacher, the poet, Sam Soloman.

This project in radical digital media literacy given the fact of fake news began in 2017 as blog posts, and then a website to hold them. It has taken many forms, engages multiple technologies, and is co-created by a large and diverse cast of contributors. The digital iterations of the project that are most frequently referred to in this book are listed below. A full and more detailed list of project iterations, and their collaborators and supports, concludes this effort.

Learning from YouTube. 2011. My born-digital "video book" about teaching and learning on corporate owned media platforms. http://vectors.usc.edu/projects/learningfromyoutube.

Online Primer on Digital Media Literacy. 2017. #100hardtruths–#fakenews. 100 blog posts by scores of scholars, activists, artists, and journalists posted over the first 100 days of the presidency of our lier-in-chief. https://scalar.usc.edu/nehvectors/100hardtruths-fakenews/index.

Fake News Poetry project website and repository. 2018-ongoing. Holds the poems, images, and ephemera from all workshops. http://fakenews-poetry.org.

10 Tries, 100 Poems :: Alexandra Juhasz :: Field Notes :: Fake News Poetry Workshops as Radical Digital Media Literacy. 2018. Blog posts by workshop leaders reflecting on the processes, outcomes, and pedagogies of their unique workshops published online by The Operating System & Liminal Lab. https://medium.com/the-operating-system/10-tries-100-poems-alexandra-juhasz-field-notes-fake-news-poetry-workshops-as-radical-ee2408808403.

Podcast. *We Need Gentle Truths for Now.* Summer 2021. 18 episodes written and performed in Covid-19 lockdown and Black Lives Matter protest. We engage in radical digital media literacy by enjoying a bite of education and a bit of poetry, creating humane responses to fake news and social media in the era of Covid-19. https://shows.acast.com/we-need-gentle-truths-for-now.

Foreword

Tara McPherson

I have written this foreword a thousand times.

I just wrote this foreword today.

I will write this foreword soon, perhaps tomorrow.

I am not sure I remember how to write at all as I, we, the luckier ones, find ourselves emerging from the darker pandemic days, days still uncertain, still rimmed by the brutalities of despots and liars, still filled to the brim with untruths, half-truths, bald-faced lies. Throughout my life, I have often sought my truths in words, both the ones I write and the ones I read. In my professional life as an academic, those words are scholarly, typically feminist, and anti-racist media theory. But my earliest truths were fictions, primarily the novels I have devoured every month since I first got a library card at 8 years old. I have always known that truth exceeds fact, that truth can fly free from evidence and soar beyond news. Truth can be weighted with footnotes, but it can also rise, lofted by the imagination.

During the height of the pandemic, I also forgot how to read. My novel reading sputtered out. For sixteen long months, I could not focus my attention on the form that had long sustained me, mapping the contours of my thinking and being. As a department chair, I was caught in frantic cycles of work, efforts that were constantly being redone and coming undone, but my mind could not enter the relational space of pleasure that reading fiction requires of me. As we endured, my attention had no duration. I turned to poetry, finding a language that better suited my fractured, iterative daily rhythms. In poetry, I could again flow into relation, seeking both truths and soothing. I could feel the words again, moving in and through language, if still briefly.

As I turned to poems, I was accessing something Alexandra (Alex) Juhasz already knew when she sculpted and refined her poetry workshops years earlier. She references these insights in the opening words to this volume, quoting Anne Waldman and Eileen Myles. She urges us to "keep the world safe for poetry," spouting forth the pure waters of the poetic form. She reminds us to *heed the poet's call.* Our world sorely needs both words and truths, and we need them swelling, growing, pulsing, fostering a vibrant communal life full of experimental and resistant forms. The powers of poetry escape the confines of computational logics and remind us of each other.

I found solace in poetics during a pandemic that closed me off from other beloved forms of fiction as well as from much of my fleshy community, but Alex had already surmised a world to come, building a praxis for communion and community through and across difference before the pandemic was upon us. She knew what we would need before we needed it, bringing it into being through force of will, radical love, stubbornness, and perhaps a dose of smart ass-ery. She was navigating the viral, limning its fault lines and its limits, long before any of us had heard of the virus Covid-19.

Alex has always been prescient like that. From her engagements with video and public access television during the early years of the AIDS crisis to her pedagogical and scholarly investigations of YouTube beginning in 2007, she embraces new platforms with a fierce criticality and a vital creative energy. She is eager to understand emergent media practices through a deep material engagement with their forms and networks, but her pursuits are never in service of the new technologies themselves. Rather, Alex takes up such forms in order to test their limits, to highlight their corporate logics, and to pursue the nascent possibilities that might linger behind shiny, slick interfaces. Alex once wrote a "book" about YouTube *by making videos,* producing a digital object that was meant to explore the constraints of the then emerging platform by modeling different ways of doing the digital at the same time. That project refracted many of the through lines of Alex's creative and scholarly life: she works in deep collaboration with others (in the case of *Learning from YouTube* with the Scalar team I founded and, in particular, with our creative technologist, Craig Dietrich with whom she continued to collaborate on her Scalar site for this project, #100hardtruths-#faknenews); she fearlessly dives in, proceeding iteratively and recursively; she learns from doing, melding theory and practice again and again; she has fun; her doing serves others, always aligning her praxis with her desire for a more just world. Such concerns — collaboration, iteration, creativity, pleasure, and ethics — ripple across the pages of this book, illustrating a profound commitment to fostering and inhabiting creative community.

While we've been taught to call our digital media "social," Alex hails us to turn away from that corporate lie, drawing us back toward embodied, local gatherings. She insists on a community beyond the digital that focuses on process, on messiness, on imperfection. Our phones lie to us. We know this in our bones. Alex offers an "invitation and invocation to participate" without the mediation of our apps. She shows us how to come together to build temporary refuge, spaces that can counter the internet's virile virality. The project cannot, of course, escape the digital, and Alex is no Luddite. She instead points us toward small spaces of respite and enclosure that transcend the obsessions and endless churn of algorithms. Such spaces value context, connection, creativity, and community.

The poems collected here loop back to specific places, bearing traces of their geographic origins. These spatial references bring contour to poetic form, creating a texture that both includes and exceeds the words that comprise each entry. Community shimmers along the edges of the stanzas, peeking from behind the lines, looking back at us in the volume's photographs that capture hugs, stares, hands, couches, tensions, pleasures, dykes, desks, sanctuaries, screens, and thighs.

My Phone Lies to Me gifts us a selection of poems but also a way of doing poetry, offering the technique of the workshop as a lively way to be. The workshop is a methodology that privileges the local, the small, and the connected, carving out spaces to see and to hear and to feel and, crucially, to make, even as the workshop as process is more important than the thing that gets made. That is not to say the poems collected here are not beautiful, sad, hopeful, poignant, and powerful. They are at once those things and also tangible artifacts of gatherings now gone but still resonating, connecting poets and activists across space and time. The pages of this book and the process Alex has designed spin webs of reference, picking up a poem from one place and reimagining it down the road, across the pond, in a different time zone. The echoes of connection ripple across this slim volume, linking Vancouver to Amsterdam, Hanover to Los Angeles, me to you. (You can find my picture here. I am not lying. I am always learning from and with Alex.)

Alex and her collaborators offer us sage advice: sit side by side, inhabit your discomfort but also your flesh, make things, shake things, move your body. *"Aerobicize with me,"* says Sam Solomon. In a world where our screens and devices ask always to be refreshed, here we find a pause that slows down and is refreshing, moving to a rhythm that isn't torqued for maximum speed and productivity. Hang here for a while. Host a workshop. Write a poem. Find a gentle truth that may set you free.

The truth is the space we fight to shape (M. Astley) as we defer our own undoing (Alexandra Juhasz).

I will never finish this foreword but will still go forward. I am reading novels again. We will be novel again.

Introduction

My Phone Lies to Me [Response]

My phones tells me to look at it.
It tells me there's a world inside,
But when I look away, I know that's not true.
There's a world right there.
The phone asks me to look again.
It tells me it's real.
But I ask it to speak,
To breathe,
To love,
To hate,
And it can't do that.

—James, Shamine, and Marsela

Written at a Fake News Poetry Workshop at New Utrecht High, Brooklyn, NY, on May 20, 2019, as a response to a poem of the same name written by Sam Solomon at a workshop at the University of Sussex in Falmer, England in 2018. A video of the same name was also produced by a group of students at New Utrecht High and can be seen in the section Video Poems and Writing on fakenews-poetry.org. It is considered in the We Need Gentle Truths For Now *episode, "The Real Internet is a Fake," which is also the name of the first #100hardtruths–#fakenews.*

A significant body of my academic and artistic work, made over a great many years, focuses on things fake: movies, YouTube videos, internet infrastructures, "social" media. *My phones tells me to look at it. / It tells me there's a world inside.* I have done much of my looking with others, like Brooklyn high school students, James, Shamine, and Marsela (in this case relying on their first names only. As is true for all of the poems that follow from a variety of workshops, poems' authors' names have been self- or teacher-determined). Together, we look, write, read, and share as forms of teaching and learning by way of art and technology. As serious as I know this work is, I have for over a decade mostly laughingly called myself one of the world's "earliest and preeminent YouTube scholars," echoing the mocking claims made about me in viral media concerning my early 2000s research and pedagogy on and about YouTube at the birth of this new "internet nation-state" (from the title of #100hardtruths #9). In the right setting, like my previous born-digital "video-book," *Learning from YouTube* (MIT Press, 2011), you might catch me ironically preening about this lofty stature in a sea of digital detritus.

More seriously, I really have thought hard about and made fakes. I produced and performed in a notable fake documentary, *The Watermelon Woman* (dir. Cheryl Dunye, 1996); co-edited a book on the subject with Jesse Lerner, *F is for Phony: Fake Documentary and Truth's Undoing* (University of Minnesota Press, 2001); and wrote extensively on the undoing or remaking of the fake-real binary as a definitive structure and practice of YouTube, as well as the internet in which it sits, in writing and media I made with my college students and everyday YouTubers, *Learning from YouTube*. A scholarly book about novel, creative, feminist, queer, and indeterminate approaches to this crisis (including poetry), co-authored with Nishant Shah and Ganaele Langlois, *Really Fake* (University of Minnesota Press and meson press, 2021) is the most recent companion to this effort; and I made an eighteen-episode podcast about poetry, fake news, pedagogy, and Black Lives Matter during the Covid-19 lockdown, *We Need Gentle Truths for Now* (2020) with a host of scholars, poets, and friends. Given how it morphs and memes, I keep researching, listening, and writing about the digital-real, often although not always, with others. *The phone asks me to look again. / It tells me it's real. / But I ask it to speak.* I learn with James, Shamine, and Marsela, who wrote their poem — which provides the title of this book as well as keen insight into fakes — at a Fake News Poetry Workshop at New Utrecht High in Brooklyn in 2019. While the internet can't breathe or love or hate, we can and do, there and elsewhere.

I seek, make, learn from, and activate media sites for robust, critical, and self-aware engagement and interaction. For nearly thirty years I have made and taught about radical art production in the name of social justice including bodies of work about AIDS, Black lesbians, queer family, and other causes that matter to me and my world. I call this my media praxis: the wholistic linking of media production, theory, and history with stated goals of self- and world-changing. My affirmative project seeks to arm communities with whom I share in struggle with the empowering tools of "media literacy": skills to make, read, and distribute our own media, as well as to challenge and better the images and ideas circulated against our interests and in large volume by the corporate or dominant media.

Then came November 2016 and the election of the 45th president of the United States of America. In the face of this shattering news, unsure how I could help or even participate productively, in early 2017 I devoted myself to a personal project. I would blog once a day about fake news for the administration's first 100 days. My idea was to counter the new president's use of media to sow confusion, distrust, and disorientation with my own 100-point primer on digital media literacy that offered, instead, a steady, reasoned set of ideas and resources written and made by myself and many others, all seeking clarity and justice. That became #100hardtruths–#fakenews, a forerunner to and resource for what would become my Fake News Poetry Project.

Activity alert at 5:27 p.m.: gather 13 social network comments.

1. I used to spend half my life chasing networks. Now with YouTube, I've swapped that time for time to create.
2. Started from 0, now I'm at 19k. Next I'll be at 100k.
3. ... even a whit the beauty she leaves behind like her eternal, up to now, shadow.
4. Dude I have no idea how I got here but I'm glad I did
5. Only Beethoven and Bach come close.
6. Context: a knightship is a glider (a structure that translates itself across the Life grid periodically)
[*ran out of time*]

—Kyle Booten

Written following a Fake News Poetry script produced at the Ammerman Center workshop on Feb. 15, 2018, referring to #100hardtruths #76: Learn what happens when you type a letter on your keyboard, contributed to that effort by Eileen Clancy.

I used to spend half my life chasing networks. Did I have something helpful to contribute or do beyond either putting my body on the street with others or placing my associated clicks and words and images on to the internet? ... *even a whit the beauty she leaves behind like her eternal, up to now, shadow.* Fake news designed to divert our attention was growing at a viral rate. The new president added to this confusion and power by using the term loosely to demean anything he perceived as an assault against him and his sordid depictions of reality. The mainstream and social media took up the term to focus on how the election (and related crimes) had been affected by falsities spread by malevolent forces, including Russia, and less self-aware agents, including bots, algorithms, and echo chambers built from our own likes, hashtags, and re-posts.

I felt both compelled and qualified to act in a time of confusion, despair, and self-criticism. I knew about fakes, and I had spent a long career within various fields of academics, activists, and artists who, like me, were committed to understanding how media works as part of a larger project of citizenship and commitment to social justice. But as was true for many of my peers at this moment, much of what we had learned and taught about digital media literacy felt inadequate to this threat which seemed to demand new analyses, approaches, and correctives.

I thought hard about the problem of digital media literacy given the fact of fake news alongside many others, and over his first 100 days (from January 20–April 29, 2017). I did indeed blog 100 times. I called each of these posts a "#100hardtruth." At about day fifty, with the assistance of designer Craig Dietrich, they were built into a stand-alone website: #100hardtruths–#fakenews. All told, the 100 #hardtruths hold a great many things: my own or other people's responses to daily offenses, diverse analytical frameworks that are useful to understand these onslaughts, and lists of additional resources made available for more reading and research. More than half of the #100hardtruths point to work written by others, colleagues from a variety of fields who were contemporaneously attempting to understand, combat, or teach about the crisis of fake news and related media literacy as it was unfolding. Written online as a Scalar book, its Table of Contents includes pathways through fifty-nine of the #100hardtruths that were authored or inspired by the work of others. A vast array of information accumulated across these blog posts, and this considered a vast array of forms: online apps, journalism, scholarly writing, art videos, photographs, activist interventions, and poetry. Collected on my primer on digital media literacy were humans' and institutions' real-time attempts to make sense of madness. The site remains a useful compendium of interdisciplinary expressions of keen knowledge, helpful resources, thoughtful tools, and desperate attempts to respond to the escalating assaults over the first 100 days. Since then, with the help of Xiomara Rodriguez and the words of many more contributors, I've added to it, building in more poems, videos, podcast episodes, and other responses to the 100 original #hardtruths that have been made after the fact, as the project continues and bleeds into other media and forms (poems, and this book, for example).

The #100hardtruths–#fakenews primer is a well-designed online receptacle holding a great deal of valuable information for teaching and learning. But in this form — which I grew to understand as its own tower of babble (see #100hardtruths #87), one built in response to more of the same — the resources I had written, gathered, and cobbled into one place online remained (or became newly) hard to navigate. Once completed, I found the primer to be too dense and perhaps holding too much jargon and even just stuff, regardless of how good, to be as usable as I hoped it could be given all the communities curious about and committed to understanding and rectifying the indignities of fake news. Even more critically, the project had confirmed for me how fully implicated in fake news we are whenever we attend to it online; my first adage of many to be derived and dissected in the project, "Fake news r us." The primer's digital home leaves it (and us) complicit in the larger problem: mining and getting lost in digital minutiae (written by others); using digital formats for our exchanges (which tend to get nasty or stay stupid); engaging in digital ways of being (which move us toward isolation, self-hatred, doubt, despair, or conflict); while seeking short-term (word- or image-bound) fixes to problems that can't be thought through or answered in this way. Learning hard things over the long term is part of the solution (i.e., #100*hard*truths). Ease, simplicity, speed, condensation, what I called "slogans" in *Learning from YouTube,* are definitive of the internet vernaculars, structures, and norms that are part of the problem. I knew there must be more that I could do to participate in and understand internet culture in ways that might work to undo, remake, or better it.

I really wanted to learn with others about what *radical* digital media literacy might look like given the fact of fake news. Perhaps I could rally new communities, forms, and formats of energy and assistance. I wanted to be digitally productive rather than reactive.

Choose to be digitally productive rather than reactive

reactive
Is being proactive in sharing your Truths
Are not False
Proven to be questionable
The Hangman has lost her noose
Be careful.
"the problem now with the internet is that the past is always there..." as
you grow up you are going to
change

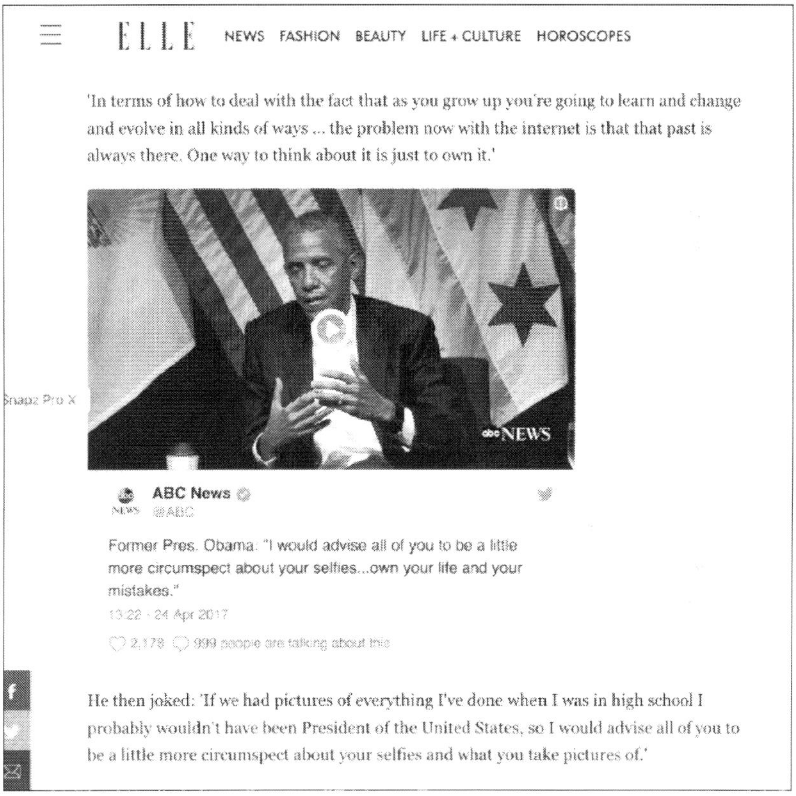

lives
Forever
oceans are drowning in plastic

A response to #100hardtruths #55: Choose to be digitally productive rather than reactive, written as an exquisite corpse poem at the workshop held at the DIGITAL EngAGEment Conference in Manhattan, NY, on May 18, 2018. Episode 12 of We Need Gentle Truths For Now, *with the same name, features Orr Menirom, and her cut-up process that generated this and other poems featured in this collection.*

My project pivoted. I wanted to create resources but also processes to understand and improve internet falsities — a way of writing, listening, engaging, and contributing differently from what we already do and know so well, and so badly, on the internet. *Reactive / Is being proactive in sharing your Truths.* All that I had known and done before, including the online primer, was useful, just nothing like enough. *Lives / Forever / oceans are drowning in plastic.* I had conceived of the primer foremost as an act of civic engagement qua pedagogy, art-making, and community-building. But it stayed stagnant and only online. Meanwhile, it turns out that many of its #hardtruths had discussed or were even written as poetry, including my own final #100hardtruths: "Speak and spell, teach and tell, count and swell," which began with two poetic responses:

> Poets are summoned to a stronger imagination of language and humanity in a time of new and radical Weathers. White House Inc. is the last gasp of the dying Confederacy, but its spectacle is dangerous and addictive so hold onto your mind. Fascism loves distraction. Keep the world safe for poetry. Open the book of love and resistance. Don't tarry! (Anne Waldman, *Resist Much, Obey Little: Inaugural Poems to the Resistance*)

> we can't build a wall. we can only spout pure water again and again and drown his lies (Eileen Myles, *Resist Much, Obey Little: Inaugural Poems to the Resistance*)

How could I help summon poetry, *spout pure water* with others, given that I wasn't a poet? I conceived of the idea of workshops, co-organized with local poets, in places of their choosing. They could teach and tell; together we could speak and swell. We would make use of different formats, processes, and places than those that had been built and abetted by digital and social media. *Proven to be questionable / The Hangman has lost her noose / Be careful.* We would use our time together to think about fake news, poetry, and each other. We would write and read other's thoughts and feelings about fake things. We would seek to better express our keen knowledge, concern, and curiosity about a host of interrelated phenomena. We would do better in response to a crisis of our own making, and thereby perhaps defer our own undoing.

Anomalous

I am not supposed to be beautiful. If I am famous — a singer, an actor, maybe I can be pretty, maybe striking, maybe exotic. Because then I am an exception, I can break the rules. But me — plain, ordinary, everyday woman — no. I am not supposed to be beautiful.

If I am beautiful, equations don't square. If I am beautiful, where is the logic in keeping me hidden, selling me relaxers and skin-lightening creams. If I am beautiful, there is no need to cover my thick, nappy hair, hide me in the kitchen, shame me for my hips and thighs, mock me for my lips.

So I am not supposed to be beautiful. That is the forever domain of light women, of white women, of any-shade-brighter-than-mine women.

My neighbor, walking home beside me in sixth grade, told me I was pretty. He said it with a clearly confused wonder, "You're actually pretty," he'd said. He couldn't understand it. But then he worked it out, settled me into a category that explained how I wasn't ugly: "It must be because you don't have those nasty liver lips like most Black people do."

Because even at 11 years old, he understood that I wasn't supposed to be beautiful, that beauty in my face was some dangerous anomaly, some breaking down of natural law.

I am not supposed to be beautiful. My mother and her mother and all of her foremothers — we, none of us, are supposed to be beautiful.

And yet. And yet. And yet.

— Stacie Evans

Written at a Fake News Poetry Workshop on Race in the Media, Brooklyn, NY, May 5, 2018 as a loose response to #100hardtruths #77: Expose the costs and histories of freedom, written by Gabrielle Foreman for that effort. A video-poem was made based on these previous engagements at the New Haven, CT workshop. Two We Need Gentle Truths For Now *episodes grew from these interactions and ruminations: episode 3, "Black Lives Matter: Expose the Costs and Histories of Freedom," focusing on the ideas of Foreman and her poet father, Kent Foreman and episode 6, "Black Lives Matter: Make Manifest the Contingencies of the Social," where Evans discusses her poem with scholar, Laura Wexler.*

For the next year and until this day, I co-organized more than twenty Fake News Poetry Workshops around the world and with diverse communities in which small groups of people listened to and learned from each other. Each workshop was different, but in all of them we thought about and then communicated our own internet truths. *I am not supposed to be beautiful.* After learning from others, in a shared context and with the permissions allowed by poetic license — vernaculars and modes of being and communicating outside of internet-speak and our internet-home — we represented our own #hardtruths. *My mother and her mother and all of her foremothers — we, none of us, are supposed to be beautiful.*

This is radical digital media literacy: engaging small groups of participants in local, embodied artmaking concerning our discrete personal and community truths, others' precious ideas and art, aligned with research about social media and fake news, and held within an ethical and known context. *If I am beautiful, equations don't square.* While I developed no equations, I was doing a lot of counting (100), consolidating, and list making. Five overarching adages came from my work on the primer:

- *fake news r us:* We are implicated by, produce, and circulate this digital media crisis whenever we study, teach, or try to fix it.
- *virality is virility:* Beneath fake news lies a potent mix of internet-fueled falsity and masculine grandiosity, which results in real-world bellicosity.
- *art answers to phony questions:* Trying to determine truth using digital media leads to the he-said/he-said rabbit hole in which we find ourselves. Departing from evidence-based, indexically linked practices into realms of truth-telling verifiable by different logics might get us out.
- *our internet truths trump media lies:* We must name, share, and honor our own lived experiences within social media as another form of honesty in desperate times. Let's first do this together offline, where we live, work, struggle, and learn.
- *heed the poet's call:* Poetry, a time-honored literary form of truth-telling outside the logics of indexical mediation, is a literacy practice well-suited to this crisis.

Three of these adages—*fake news r us, art answers to phony questions,* and *heed the poet's call*—would inspire my own next steps, Fake News Poetry Workshops, bringing people together to generate conversation, community, and art about the connections between social media, verification tools, and lived truth. I travel somewhere and, working with a local poet or poets and their communities, develop a workshop in which participants generate poems on the theme of fake news after talking, listening, researching, and feeling, together, in a real place and shared time. To counter digital media's reliance on the driving logic of scale, workshops stay small and local.

This book presents some of the over 100 (and counting!) poems created during those sessions. But as moving, eloquent, and useful as the poems may be—and I invite you to indulge in and learn from them—enjoying and learning from them is only a part of this book's point. This project is foremost an invitation and invocation for you to participate, with others, in an experiment in knowing and working with the internet differently. Thus, my conclusion will offer a brief introduction to some of the theoretical thinking undergirding the project as well as a twenty-step process to create your own poetry and workshops.

Fake News Poetry Workshops; this book about them and the many poems, connections, and interactions engendered, are all ways to counter the internet's dominant and dominating modes and values, to fight the corrupt ways of being and knowing that use digital media to create, fuel, and weaponize fake news and the people, machines, and corporations that make it. Yes, this project is primarily interested in contravening the logics of the internet that have fanned fake news into the conflagration it is today, even as it is not against or outside of it.

Thus, much (more) of this project also sits and changes on the internet: the digital media literacy primer, #100hardtruths–#fakenews, ready to be taught and read; an elegant "book" of those #hardtruths, also designed by Craig Dietrich, that can be enjoyed as a PDF or paper volume; another website, fakenews-poetry.org, a beautiful repository that holds all the poems as well as their documentation as photos and other ephemera; a third effort, "10 Tries: 100 Poems," published on the Operating System & Liminal Lab's website in their Field Notes section in 2018, which generously allowed many of the collaborating poets to write about their workshops and responses to the project; and a podcast series from 2020, *We Need Gentle Truths for Now,* with eighteen short episodes connecting the processes, poems, and digital media literacy of the project with Covid-19 lockdown and its concurrent Black Lives Matter protests. Of course, this book of poems can be enjoyed digitally as a PDF. But better yet, we imagine it printed out and held in your hands as a book on paper. These many self-reflexive movements from paper to digital to person and back again are part of the radical digital media literacy.

Whatever their delivery format, the poems are most useful when contextualized. As is true of any pile of things, they can be grouped in many ways, each revealing different orientations. Indeed, they align within assorted logics in their many media homes: by the physical locations of each workshop on fakenews-poetry.org; by their alignment to the original #100hardtruths on the online, digital media primer, which was itself created chronologically. Here, they are loosely organized to my five adages. I have also linked each of the poems here to one of my original #100hardtruths. Some were explicitly written about or connected to a #100hardtruths, others I linked together after the fact, building new connections allowing for other paths for thinking about fake news.

In this effort, each poem is also accompanied by brief contextual details about where, when, and with who it was written. The diversity, specificity, and variety of the lived reality of the time, labor, place, and enthusiasms of the project's many participants and places are part of its values. Along this vein, I also explain briefly how each poem, as part of the workshop process, refers to or builds from others' previous work, linking it to more digital and material iterations, thereby modeling and extending an anti-meme logic. Our internet things are considered, passed on, and reused with care because they are esteemed as the real effort of another known person from a named place and time. I do my best to detail these many stops, starts, and hand-offs to reveal that logic and its linked processes.

I have worked hard to move placed-based knowledge and encounters from one part of the world to another, and from one format to another, and from one person to another, for personal, theoretical, and political reasons. Poems have helped. They hold traces of the varied workshops, enjoyed as local interactions between people and internet-held knowledge, as well as each writer's unique wisdom spoken with her own beauty. From their words we can encounter and counter the structuring logics of fake news. The poems teach, and in so doing prove that artmaking, connected to our experiences of self, community, place, and truth, can be one small part of a shared way out of, or perhaps through, our terrible troubles.

However: no news is good news. These poems and this publication are not a solution but rather an invitation and an invocation to act and do a little differently — to better the internet and better ourselves. *What a lousy host.*

No News Is Good News

I had my face pressed up so hard
against the glass
my nose spread across my face
like wings
I was trying to catch a glimpse
of a dead body on the newsroom floor
the one from this morning
or perhaps the one from the day before
Couldn't find one tho'
Somehow no news is good news
They said
"You won't find it there
only by the candle light vigil
adjacent to the corner store
by way of the shrieking mother"
then I started thinking
about how the rotting flesh would stink up the place
and maybe one of them would vomit on live T.V.
like any other day
I asked the mother if that's what she wanted
She replied,
"No news has ever been good news"
Not here, I thought
especially not here
I turned on the radio
hoping to escape on the radio waves
listen to a story or two
instead I heard the ramblings of an indignant man
What a lousy host
Is no news good news?
I called in immediately
got put on hold
so I counted all the money I had in my pocket
he answered and I said
"I have 22 dollars
and I'll give you each one
to stop all that damn
rabid
foamy-mouth
sobbing"
That day I found out
That no news really is good news

—Kai Mora

Written after the Fake News Poetry Workshop at LaGuardia Community College in Queens, NY, on April 24, 2018, as a response to #100hardtruths #57: Most Americans may conclude he's a fake president, which was written by the editorial staff of The Wall Street Journal *in "A President's Credibility." A video-poem was adapted from this poem at the New Haven workshop, New Haven, CT, Nov. 3, 2018.*

LaGuardia Community College student, Kai Mora, shares my belief that fake news and its immoral logics support and engender violence: virality is virility. *I was trying to catch a glimpse / of a dead body on the newsroom floor / the one from this morning / or perhaps the one from the day before.* Similarly, Harvey P., a cognitively disabled adult poet and performer, shares my belief that "our internet truths trump media lies." Their poems, along with the many others included here and yours that will also connect and build, offer worthier ways to learn, speak, listen, and know about fake news.

Technology can be used for good things and bad things

Technology is a Weapon
Technology can be used for good and bad things.
It can be used for creating and destroying.
We can use technology for making our lives more convenient.
It can also be used as a means of protection from evil.
Each instrument is used for a specific purpose.
It can also be used for committing and preventing crimes.
If technology is used in a bad way it can destroy the world.
We need to prevent that from happening.
We need technology so that good can triumph over evil.

— Harvey P.

Written at a Fake News Poetry Workshop with Poets of Course, in Harlem, NY, on Oct. 13, 2018. This is a loose response to #100hardtruths #91: We need the NEA and NEH to know how to imagine ourselves as a nation, which was written for that effort by Laura Wexler, feminist scholar of photography and American Studies who later participated with Stacie Evans in We Need Gentle Truths For Now *episode 8, "Black Lives Matter: Make Manifest the Contingency of the Social." They had first met and worked together at the video-poetry workshop in New Haven, CT.*

Fig. 1. A fragment written at the Toronto Workshop. My guess is that it is by the workshop's host, T.L. Cowan, who wrote #100hardtruths–#fakenews #93: "citation is not enough." But who knows? In any case, a party followed, and that seemed just right.

I hope the poems will feed you. *Each instrument is used for a specific purpose.* But this guide is not really about reading and the comforts of sitting.

Our shared purpose will be to contribute to, counter, and improve our contemporary media state, and then pass it on gently to others who want to engage differently. I seek your doing, through different logics of ownership, comfort, and connection, contra but also about the internet: being and making together in known places and times while taking on care and attention: not just citing, but also sitting; not just reading but also writing; not just working but also partying.

fake news r us

we are implicated by, produce, and circulate this crisis

whenever we study, teach, or try to fix it

Trump is Our Rightful Internet Present

by Maria Z.

#100hardtruths #3: Trump is our rightful internet president

Trump is always on the internet.
Trump is on Twitter always lying.
He cheated on his wives and he is in office?
Trump does not tell the truth and God will judge his heart.
Why doesn't Trump man up and tell the truth?
How dare you Trump, cover up your thighs?
You are a lying, adulterous man who broke one of the Ten Commandments. It's
Thou shalt not commit adultery.
Trump you must confess on what you did.
If you don't confess your sin how will you live yourself?
Trump you can't handle the truth.

Written at the Poets of Course workshop, Manhattan, NY, Oct. 2, 2018.

We can learn to practice truth every day

Anonymous poetry fragment

#100hardtruths #10: YouTube is a performatively self-aware political-economy

We can learn to
practice truth every day,
to codeswitch, to
think, to ask, refuse
start over, triangulate,
disbelief, know when we
are being dominated and, if
we are fortunate, lucky, careful, heedful
to move

Written at the Toronto workshop, Toronto, Ontario, March 17, 2018.

I choose to believe

by Emily Holmes

#100hardtruths #11: Real apologies for #fakenews aggravate its symptoms

I choose
to believe
that you are not lying to me
when you claim to trace your tracks
See here
when I seemed to be there
but I was not
I was elsewhere
doing something Valid
You say
in the same state of seeming
And I do not see
any deference.

Written at the University of Sussex workshop, Falmer, England, March 19, 2018.

These Bitter Lies

by Olympia Miccion

#100hardtruths #14: Skepticism is a weapon

How broken has my free thought become.
Sometimes my false perceptions (gifted from the internet)
Are more twisted than sprained ankles.
Leg casts and broadcasts.
My head needs crutches, sometimes.
I double and triple A check myself.

But the Truth is hard to uncover.
The Truth is as easily distorted as emptied lemons,
Looking crushed from dirty fingers.
Congressmen
Curl up like lying tongues.
Their lips pucker when they are met with facts
That don't offer wiggle room.
So they turn to twitter—
Use the virtual world as a buffer.

The day 45 was elected,
I collected suicide hotlines in my palms.
Today,
They tear through my hands like thumbtacks.
We yell of unrest
Of fake news,
Of untruth
Yet they just put a pin in it.
Thumbtack my freethought.

My mom warns me, to be careful of what I put on the internet,
Because it stays there forever.

How do we keep forgetting and forgiving this buffer?
Outrage is easily forgotten,
We toss out rotten lemons
Without targeting rotten trees,
How do we keep letting aggressions
And hate
Spark outrage and then die out as easily
as those embers were made.

I still know a couple suicide hotlines by heart.
I still try and turn lemons into lemonade.
We will not sit quietly,
And be forced into drinking
These lies

Anymore.

Written at the Get Lit workshop, Los Angeles, CA, Oct. 13, 2018. #100hardtruths #14 refers to the City University of New York's Graduate School of Journalism's LibGuide, "Fact Checking, Verification, and Fake News."

How do you Authenticate a Person?

by Leroy J.

#100hardtruths #6: Today's fixes to fake news are bogus

Technology is a weapon, a knife. A gun.
How do you authenticate a person? You pay them.
The truth is... candy? I don't know.

Written at the Poets of Course workshop, Manhattan, NY, Oct. 2, 2018.

Confidence, anxiety, alienated

by LaGuardia Community College students listing words for their thoughts and responses to fake news and... a feeling, something to change, a technology, and a site on their own body where they feel all this most

#100hardtruths #7: Skeptical interaction with the digital is critical for democracy

Stomach neck
Confidence, anxiety, alienated.
Stomach neck
Insecure excited
Stomach neck
Anxiety depressed.
Stomach neck
Depressed annoyed.
Insecure anxiety.

Joyous.
Frustrated.
Pressure.
Half-alive.
Getaway stress.

Confused targeted.
Occupied.
Less judgment.
Open-mindedness.
More connected
More acceptance
Less sensitive the world.

The world.
The government.
More free peace.
I hope I can speak more.
Understand each other better.
I just want everyone to be successful.
To move beyond the easy place.
Better listening.
All humans enjoy respect.
To make the world better for everyone.
Happiness and peace. Free speech. Peace.

Snapchat. Instagram and snapchat.
Cellphone. Instagram. My laptop.

Instagram Facebook
YouTube. YouTube.
Wii chat Wii chat snapchat.
Playstation 4. Laptop.

Phone
Book
Cellphone phone all of those
My surrounding
Phone.
Mouth feelings eyes.
Stomach stomach
Brain heart forehead
Ears eyes brain
Heart hands wrist
Sternum
My throat
Brain
My head my heart
My liver
Arm.

Written at the LaGuardia Community College workshop, Queens, NY, April 24, 2018.

Voyeurism is me you

by Annie Dobson

#100hardtruths #17: Barack Obama says, "we won't know what to protect"

Voyeurism is me you
eating popcorn eating skittles watching
The Latest Bad Thing unravel
You like to say
There has been another school shooting in America
& read me the details off your phone
17 confirmed dead, suspect arrested
little newsreader
You said you wanted to die in a big american swimming pool
I said I wanted to speak truthfully with you in a swimming pool cafe
I like to say
We have to get married now anyway
because we stayed up together
eating crisps eating leftover pasta watching
the 2016 election results
My future children, in their perfect television accents will ask me
Where were you when you heard? What world did you hear it in?
& I want that moment to be perfect

Written at the University of Sussex workshop, Falmer, England, March 19, 2018.

#Science is Real

by José G.

#100hardtruths #35: Science is real

Science is challenged by religious people
they have their own ideas about science
That is not fact, it's fiction
Science is challenged by politicians.
They deny science,
that global warming is real.
They want to destroy the planet,
make money,
they don't care about the future.
Science is challenged by stupid people
who think the Earth is flat.
Old science stupidity
You try to explain the fact,
they don't want to believe it.
The proof is in the pudding
My science is challenged by people that are too stubborn to understand
I am not stupid
I am a smart person
I am not a rare unicorn
"Oh my God! A Latino person who is smart!"
"Oh my God! A disabled person who is smart!"
I have a disability, I am not stupid

Written at the Poets of Course workshop, Manhattan, NY, Oct. 2, 2018.

Time Tracks (excerpts)
A Poetry Walk from Ditmas Park to the Interference Archive

by Gavin McCormick and Alexandra Juhasz
generated by a script from Lisa Moren and Maro Perez

#100hardtruths #36: History is real

1. Woman holds balloons.
Orange cat.
Cantaloupe, smashed.
A mom chastises Felix (age 8?):
"It reflects badly on you, and it reflects badly on me. Like who wants to invite Felix?
And then, what kind of mother is she?"
Smear of a woman through opaque window.
Enjoying the snow? "Enjoying a smoke!"

1A. balloon bouquet
poor Felix
you're embarrassing me.
Enjoying the snow?
Enjoying my smoke.

....

3. Juifs Pour Jesus.
4U2NV.com
Remember We Are Made of Dust, And To Dust We Shall Return
Canyon walls of brick apartments. Spanish conversations.
Single skein of razor wire.

3A. Cavern of walls I often slide through
feel warm when we write.
Fakenews is built upon
denuding our dignified upstanding
neighbors simply because of
words. Frailty, varied taste.

....

6. The park's painterly welcome: Skeleton branches lace atop a slate sky rippled
with bruise-black cloud crests.
Scores of skaters trace one rink,
Zamboni smoothes a second.
Smell of frying meat.
Whinging toddler strains in a stroller; stoic father, grey whiskered, miles back,
pushes on.

6A. I can remember holding my little children
with a sense memory better than
any photo.
The body, my body, is this sort
of private truth holder
and generator.

....

8. Uphill seems longer.
Bikers, walkers, a steady stream.
Skateboarder smartphone-shoots his snow-splashed descent.
Snow curtain shifts in every streetlight, thin lace to dense brocade:
We step center stage.

8A. The smartphone distraction comes too soon.
But I like how the stop
makes a lock.
So much snow on my face
shattered and magnified by
street lights.
I miss my son
when the world presents
sheer delight.
Love and belonging and longing
are outside capitalism.

...

11. Stop for a slice: 100 minutes in, a mile yet to walk.
TV on mute: Dead baby found in Astoria Park.
One to three inches expected.
Somber Melania visits Florida.
Students rally against gun violence.
Storm warning.

11A. My #100hardtruths–#fakenews project
tracked outside falsities
alongside inner reactions
now public.
But not stimuli of the
earth; my body; yours.

...

13. Time has bent, slowed, sped. Walk for 5 minutes, write for 2, one space then another, stop, start, a moment or an age. Tracking time has fixed us to and loosed us from. We arrive: 10 minutes early.

Written in Brooklyn, NY, from a script written at the Ammerman Center workshop, Feb. 15, 2018. #100hardtruths #16 refers to ideas generated by Alexandra Hidalgo in "Cámara Retórica: A Feminist Filmmaking Methodology for Rhetoric and Composition." We Need Gentle Truths For Now *episode 14, "Practice Strategic Contemplation," features Hidalgo, Juhasz, and McCormick.*

The pent present parent haven't seen nothin'

exquisite corpse poem

#100hardtruths #42: Phatic communication eases interactions but lessens information

invisible is inedible Hungry for
Truth?
Who determines what is true?
the media
The Medea
RESIST HOW WE
ARE FRAMED
to think the way we think

Made at the DIGITAL EngAGEmentConference, Manhattan, NY, May 18, 2018. #100hardtruths #42 is based on writing by Farhad Manjoo about the research of Gretchen McCulloch.

Poem (I want to live in those good old days)

by Claudia Natasha

#100hardtruths #28: Face(book?) is best for people with pale skin

I want to live in those good old days,
As soon as I leave home I begin wondering again, why,
People wander around not looking like themselves.
They go online and look up how to not look like themselves
While the other halve's creating the guides for the unseen.
I would come back home and the story is no different;
Ladies mask their faces for invalid reasons.
Recently I threw away those pencils and crayons,
Make my statement for future gentlewomen.
Oh, how I wish their time will be none like this,
Powerful, undeniable from the inside out,
Accepted as they are, professionalism redefined.
The sun has fallen, masquerade ball has arisen,
We are sitting wondering when the sun will rise again,
To return inner-peace, to restore love, to reunite
Herself with herself, beauty with purity,
The world with the truth. We still long for that revival
To wake the broken, to break the limitation
To challenge the unknown, to show.
I want to live in those good old days.

Written at the LaGuardia Community College workshop, Queens, NY, April 24, 2018. #100hardtruths #28 relies on the research of Jonathan Albright, whose "Smart.Dumb AI-Powered 'Fake News' Search Suggestions" follows the search crumbs to some pretty powerful hardtruths.

Gentle truths

Anonymous poetry fragment

#100hardtruths #43: Emotional + rational resonances needed

What if we
aimed for
gentle truths?
For now.

Written at the Toronto workshop, Toronto, Ontario, March 17, 2018.

In an ABSOLUT world/Notes on the real thing

by Angus Walker

#100hardtruths #60: How to spot a #fakenews site in 10 steps

Sifting transcendence on the shop-
floor, max out on red
carpet talk in the latest spirit
engagement, lacquer lips rainbow and
say "equality". No really say
it.
Eyes-closed dance: a platform for silent
withdrawal, redeeming chaebol
payouts down in pledge-
making, cover(t), nothing
to hide — Moon smears refresh —
official sponsors of Seoul sunrise
bloated dangle need over
waiting. Distorted marches shape
bottle and crop
barriers, fermented.

Written at the University of Sussex workshop, Falmer, England, March 19, 2018. #100hardtruths #60 was written by Claire Wardle, research director of First Draft.

A picture that will never tell my story

by Aodhan Gallagher

#100hardtruths #47: Good design and software mask bad credibility

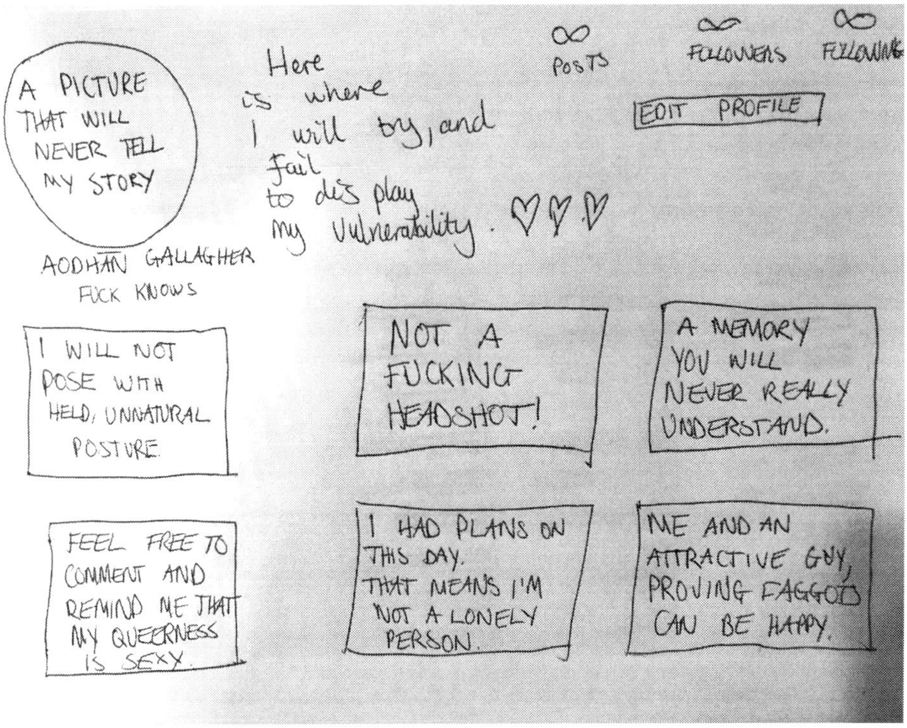

Drawn at the New York University workshop, Manhattan, NY, April 10, 2019. #100hardtruths #47 is rooted in ideas from "Facebook and Google Make Lies as Pretty as Truth: How AMP and Instant Articles Camouflage Fake News," by Kyle Chayka.

We evolved living

Spoken by a bot that was taught to be an anarchist from Portland, OR, interested in justice by Josh Urban Davis and Laura Braunstein

#100hardtruths #79: Attend to the structural problems in the platform ecosystem

We evolved living
Workers living
Natural-food living

Are workers good?

History is fighting
Workers are fighting
We began living

Workers want films
Films love quacks
Films demand Anarchists

We are living

No revolution no peace

We have attacks
We have concept
We have ignorance
We have equity

Spoken by people and a bot at the Dartmouth College workshop, Hanover, NH, Feb. 25, 2019.

Stage Fakenews Events
A poetry-writing algorithm

by Lucas Crane

#100hardtruths #84: Stage fake news events

>me: *does a thing*
You: *becomes a thing*
The internet: *says something, clutches pearls*
100 people outside in a field staring at you: *says something cheering you on*

Written at the first Fake News Poetry Workshop, held at the Ammerman Center in New London, CT, Feb. 15, 2018, and referring to #100hardtruths #84: Stage fake news events, which refers to Wait, Wait, Don't Tell Me: A Fake News Event, a digital media literacy public program featuring Brooklyn College professors M.J. Robinson and Katherine Fry, and librarian, Beth Evans.

Contrived Moment

Group poem

#100hardtruths #95: People actually DO get it

Contrived moment

Something weird happened
To TIME

AT THE BACK
OF MY TONGUE

My body is the noise of
Everything I ever liked

Mutating like slime
mould

What if the mirror
Was our own
body?

Written at the Devil's Dyke workshop, Brighton, England, March 19, 2018. #100hardtruths #95 is a contribution to the online digital media literacy primer by Antonia Juhasz, a leading energy analyst, author, and investigative journalist specializing in oil.

virality is virility

a potent mix of internet-fueled falsity, masculine grandiosity,

and resulting real-world bellicosity

undergird fake news and our efforts to understand it

Technology is a Weapon

by Gerard G.

#100hardtruths #4: The internet is built on deceptions

Technology is a weapon because it is all serious.
Between taking care of business is making you delirious.
Computer technology still searching for some information is the key to success of life.
Like everything could be serious for life.
It could be Facebook, Instagram, YouTube and more
but never post nothing in different pages before.
Never the drugs, alcohol, but it's all the same.
'Cause technology is still the same name.
Just because I need to do the hard work
don't mean I'm supposed to be the jerk.
Straight up for that I've even heard the game
of this technology thing is still the same.
Because positive choices is always on my side
But that don't mean I've lost my pride.
Losing you things could be very serious
'Cause in the real world I've never been curious.

Written at the Poets of Course workshop, Manhattan, NY, Oct. 2, 2018.

truTh
or
On the impossible quest to a life; a perperson

by William Shier

#100hardtruths #2: The fake news is real

Four abreast on a three-spine path.
From the mud redirection comes
Expectations for conceptions
For this data webbed packet territory.
the unit of now is shared in itself,
And our digital gravity
Pulls us to the dislocation.
the path-link to tomorrow never ends.
Poster on a post: equally unread
If full or blank. though this blank is lit and
Blinking small verticality —
Soon filled, now, by boxes rather than blots.
Disseminated feigned impotence of
Influence; misdirection of meaning-
Place. the upturned table may be righted,
But take away a leg? then what? What then?
take away a leg
And they'll want it to work as normal.
Legless will have always been the way.
So cord the whip
But don't
Be me.
I could do nothing.
I could be nothing.
Not-I becoming virtual

Written at the University of Sussex workshop, Falmer, England, March 19, 2018.

Fake Can be Fun

by Jack C.

#100hardtruths #9: YouTube is less platform than emerging internet nation-state

No weapons
Fake at home protection,
Homeland Security,
a camera.
Fake can be fun
In my mind I can be whatever I want to
to stop gun violence.
Climate
Warfare
dishonest politicians.
Come to agreement with President, senators and the house to stop endangering people with reckless bills.
Create a better democracy.
Give better security to the world

Written at the Poets of Course workshop, Manhattan, NY, Oct. 2, 2018.

Forget the Audience

Group poem from short fragments

#100hardtruths #15: The internet is perfect incubator for #fakenews and its material results

text buzzes & belly-rumbles

could our bodies be recording
devices that receive and share other's
truths

His behavior on Instagram
Was not far from his
reality

Written at the Devil's Dyke workshop, Brighton, England, March 19, 2018.

'Essay'

by Grace Manson

#100hardtruths #5: #fakenews is a logical outgrowth of the web's infrastructure

: that which is in medias res
is always already all-known —
a narrator gives it to you now, i.e.:
"Concept."
'Blimey! That was brilliant!' you say,
'As palatable as an apple
on a summer's day!'

Written at the University of Sussex workshop, Falmer, England, March 19, 2018, in response to #100hardtruths #94: Always look for the real thing, written by Danielle Jackson.

On Suicide Notes in Place of Passports

by Arlene Campa

#100hardtruths #20: Stress related to immigration status is one result

Migrants were born from the river's cavernous mouth
Cradled by overgrown bamboo and caña de azúcar
Ripe mango flesh dripping from our teeth
Caked in the desert's grime
Abuelita's palms fold in a symphony of praise
Her tongue wisps a language of smoke
Dense and oily, her words hang stagnant in the air
She keeps it tucked away in her diaphragm
Her lips imprinted with N-400 form
Naturalization isn't possible when your body is already considered unearthly
While burning sage to keep the spirits away
Says "Hay un remedio para todo excepto la muerte"
There is a remedy for everything except death
Someone pray for the undocumented immigrants
The infants swaddled in crimson
Product of rape by border patrol
Dehydrated bodies cremated into sand dunes
Empty water jugs rolling like tumbleweeds
We hand down heartache like heirlooms
Recuerdos of suicide notes and bullet shells
For Jose de Jesus Deniz Sahagun, 31
Screams echoing off isolated cell walls
Copper teeth grinding against the ache of vacancy
We keep mistaking detention center for death sentence
He stuffed his esophagus with socks
Attempted to take his life 3 times before
A testament to the torture behind closed doors
For Joaquin Luna, 18
Who carved out his obituary in spiral notebooks
God's greed gave him a gun
Holy bearer of bullets
Dressed in his Sunday best
He couldn't be an architect without papers
So he sprinkled blueprints with lighter fluids
Envisioned the contrast of vermillion stains on his cream shirt
Formulated the spatial composition of the bathroom and his body
Mapped out his apology in blue blood
He shot himself a week before receiving his college acceptance letter
I can't bear anymore eulogies
My bedtime stories are news reports

Sometimes I can't tell real from fake
Alternative facts scream ICE raids in the wrong places
Tombstones cluttered my closet
Each inscription with the date scraped out
From when I wanted to die at 7, 10, 13, 15
Home is only 3 letters away from homily
And I will worship every god to keep this family whole
Turn our bodies into sanctuary
Welcome to this holy house
I keep waiting for a resurrection
But the dead don't dance on the devil's back.

Written at the Get Lit workshop, Los Angeles, CA, Oct. 13, 2018.

Mash up sound-piece of "On Suicide Notes in Place of Passports" and "the go fund mes never end"

by Fabian Anthony Luna and Christiana Vivienne

#100hardtruths #13: Conservatism trends toward performance art

IN PLACE OF

I have a story to tell about myself + my surroundings — dense + oily
Her words hang stagnant in the air
I was never rejected not because God's greed gave him a gun
Not to worry what other people think of me,
but the dead don't dance on the devil's back
My identity has been changing for the better + the worst of me
I keep waiting for resurrection,
turn our bodies into sanctuary, I wanted to be by myself
Ripe mango, flesh dripping from our teeth

Written at the New York University workshop, Manhattan, NY, April 10, 2019.

Unburdened by Books

Anonymous poetry fragment

#100hardtruths #24: The 1st Amendment includes the right to receive information

Unburdened
by
books

Written at the Toronto workshop, Toronto, Ontario, March 17, 2018. #100hardtruths #24 refers to the thoughts of Chief Justices Ruth Bader Ginsburg and Elena Kagan.

for we understood their suffering, didn't we?

by Kyle Booten

#100hardtruths #33: Speed matters; there is safety in the slow

Prompt: meditate upon a line from Jennifer Moxley's Clampdown (2009), "... for we / understood their suffering, didn't we, and we / were the ones who took it upon ourselves to make it new."

We were the ones who took it upon ourselves to make it new. The time of modernism (vintage new) vs. the time of the event (actually new?) vs. the time of suffering (keep it underspecified). A new poem has the most current timestamp, though these can be forged, and the time bars scrubbed. A new poetry is exciting (desublimation) and can be explained quickly in an elevator.

Written after the Ammerman Center workshop, New London, CT, Feb. 15, 2018.

Questioning the Structure Outside the Body

Anonymous poetry fragment

#100hardtruths #48: Seek enlightenment from historical context, contemporaneous public statements, and specific sequence of events

QUESTIONING
THE STRUCTURE
OUTSIDE OF
THE BODY
BUT
WE
MUST TRUST
OUR BONES

Written at the Toronto workshop, Toronto, Ontario, March 17, 2018. #100hardtruths #48 refers to the "Order Granting Motion for Temporary Restraining Order," by Judge Derrick Watson in relation to the presidential travel ban.

Tectonic assurance is fragile ground

by Wendy Chun, Marika Cifor, Kelly Dobson, Caelin Finnigan, Jace Harrison, Hannah Holtzclaw, Ioana B. Jucan, Alexandra Juhasz, Brenda Longfellow, Sylvia Miller, Karl Surkan, Daniel Temkin, and Roopa Vasudevan

#100hardtruths #59: Silicon valley's entrepreneurial capitalism leaves rubble in its wake

Narrator: Okay, there's one person standing alone on stage, we can see their activity on the screen, and the way that they're represented on the screen is not what they actually look like.

There are ominous warnings flashing on screen that the power is about to go out. Our character is tapping on the screen.

Person: Oh no! I heard about this happening in another place, is this real?

On-Screen: No, that's not real, that's just fake news, somebody trying to fool you. That never really happens. "Do not be distracted from the truth of your own body."

Person: Did you hear that?

On-Screen: What was that? I heard something too!

Narrator: Crashing sounds, the power cuts and the screen disappears, there is the sound of feedback, then silence. ... The person is alone, they take off their headsets, they are disheveled and disoriented.

Person: What just happened? Is this real?

On-Screen: "Tectonic assurance is fragile ground."

Person: What happened to the network? They won't reboot it, what's going on?

Narrator: The voice-over actor comes on stage.

On-Screen/IRL: "The truth is the emptiness in the middle of the atom."

Person: Who are you? Did you destroy my network? Are you some kind of terrorist?

On-Screen/IRL: "The truth is the impressionability of matter, of us, the truth is a space we fight to shape."

Written at the HASTAC workshop, Vancouver, British Columbia, May 18, 2019. #100hardtruths #59 was written by digital artist Natalie Bookchin. The play uses lines from M. Astley's poem "do not be distracted from the truth," written at the University of Sussex workshop, Falmer, England. We Need Gentle Truths For Now *episode 10, "Silicon Valley's Entrepreneurial Capitalism Leaves Rubble in its Wake," creates conversation, thinking, and art between Astley and Bookchin.*

have conversations

Anonymous poetry fragment

#100hardtruths #63: The health of nations demands knowledge applied to decision-making

Have
Conversations
or
Protect your
Self from
them

Written at the Toronto workshop, Toronto, Ontario, March 17, 2018.
#100hardtruths #63 was contributed by digital humanist, Kathleen Fitzpatrick.

Information Costs Money

by José G.

#100hardtruths #67: Watch those who are monetizing their watching from the shadows

Information causes pain and suffering
Blood and Tears.
I see more suffering in people's life
and for myself
it is a wound in my soul.
Seeing everything
Fake
fake.
No truth
No honesty
Sensations that problems happen.
This country is using Facebook instead of news.
There is a Buddhist monk
says he hates Muslims.
But you are a person of faith.
Yours is a religion of love
and patience
it's understanding.
and it sickens me.
This is a person of peace and not violence.
Why are you so angry?
Angry? So angry?
You get your information from Facebook and it is not true.
He believes this news.
Not getting the facts correct.
People are not translating the news into the right language.
Only two people translating in the country
Guessing it wrong.
You say something different language in different words.
Facebook doesn't take responsibility for that.

Written at the Poets of Course workshop, Manhattan, NY, Oct. 2, 2018.
#100hardtruths #67 was contributed by digital humanist, Jacqueline Wernimont.

Call the man of the year a liar

by Mika Judge

#100hardtruths #81: Call the Man of the Year a liar

Gladly!
I would be first in line.
From the first moment of his presidency, he inflated a scraggly cloud to mammoth proportions.
It was the largest audience to witness an inauguration, period.
He is beloved, he is the prophet of all things true, period.

Some people are haters — sad! — but those who know best know him, period.
There are a lot of small things about him, but his lies are enormous. like his crowds. like his supporters. like his heart. like the coal mine he's reopening right under our feet — America, how does black lung feel?

How does it feel being cheated by a cheesy smile balanced on an emergency red tie?
How did a small loan of a million dollars become the ruining of billions of lives?
How does it feel to be led by the lovechild of racist comments on Facebook and unimaginable power?

America, get your heads out of your echo chambers.
There is more to politics than what you want to believe. There is more to know than what they show you.
Do not mistake easily obtainable for true. Do not mistake your agreement for divine approval.

Where there is doubt, there is still hope.
Period.

Written at the Get Lit workshop, Los Angeles, CA, Oct. 13, 2018. #100hardtruths #81 refers to song lyrics by Joan Baez from an anti-Trump music video she posted and shared online. We Need Gentle Truths For Now *episode 5, with this name, allows us to hear the poem read by Judge and the song sung by Baez.*

Technology is a Weapon

by Wayne B.

#100hardtruths #82: Explain your irrational destruction

The demons of dummy angels
ready to be devastated
by an army Institute University of Technology.
a SWAT team of employees
trying to destroy
a warlock military
looking in the future
of technology in a movie theater
in entertainment
fantasy under a hypnotic spell
protesters of military
technology is a weapon
a challenge of competitive Warfare
a brainstorm
that is a rainfall of knowledge
combat and tactics of survival
a military soldier in camouflage
to win the battle
and
graduate with a doctorate of weaponology
a university of pride
commitment
a guided-missile devastating and destroying
the sorcery of the uneducated.

Written at the Poets of Course workshop, Manhattan, NY, Oct. 2, 2018. #100hardtruth #82 is excerpted from "Innocence Nevermore," by poet Abraham Jesús "Tato" Livaiera: "Educate us to the rationalization of your vicious impotence / Explain your irrational destruction before the eyes of humanity." We Need Gentle Truths For Now *episode 11, with this title, features the thinking of scholar and artist Frances Negron and the poetry of Nuyorican poetry legend "Tato" Livaiera.*

I have a terrible story about social media

Group poem

#100hardtruths #83: Focus attention on the real-world applications of #fakenews

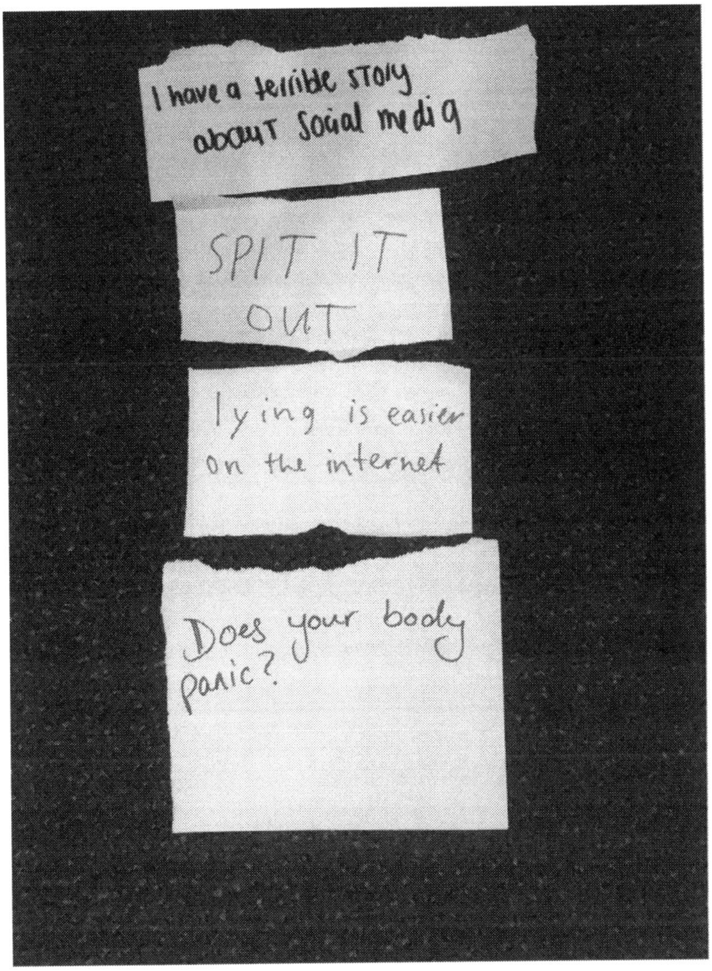

Written at the Devil's Dyke workshop, Brighton, England, March 19, 2018.

"The Beauty of Weirdos. Your Human Hope"

by Barbara Browning

#100hardtruths #98: Peace is the most powerful deterrent of all

The beauty of weirdos
Your human hope.

A song performed at the New York University workshop, Manhattan, NY, April 10, 2019, inspired by a fragment of the same name written at the Toronto workshop. Hear it online in the fakenews-poetry repository or in the final We Need Gentle Truths For Now, *episode 18, with the same name and spirit.*

Where are my perspectives?

Some lines taken from a speaking egg fed by Alexandra Juhasz, Shane Slattery-Quintanilla, and Katherine Gruzzi

#100hardtruths #100: Speak and spell, teach and tell, count and swell

where are my perspectives?
the slow process people,
the unknown cinema.

we choose the crazy?
where will we forget?
the unknown womanism farms.

estrangement are discoveries:
we hear a freedom.
how will she culminate!

Written at the ICSP workshop, Brooklyn, NY, May 20, 2019. This egg is a bot taught to speak as one with three variables: a salesperson, from San Francisco, invested in liberation. #100hardtruths #100 also invites the project's move to poetry.

Trump's
Lies
LIVE
MSNBC

uld not be
ersation
Protect your self from them

art answers to phony questions

departures from evidence-based, indexically linked practices

into realms of truth-telling verifiable by different logics

might get us out of the he-said/he-said rabbit-hole

where we currently find ourselves

What is Beauty

by Chloe Lubin

#100hardtruths #8: FAKE!

What is beauty?
Is it how long my lashes are?
Or is it the length of my natural hair?
Is it the price of my wig?
Or is it determined by the curl on my hair?
What is beauty?

You see
Beauty is what I want it to be
To me
I can choose if I wanna be ~~ugly~~ or ~~pretty~~
Because my beauty is chosen by me

It is not for you
Nor is it for the man across the street
My make up is for me because I like it
My jeans are for me
My ass is for me
My body is with me thus it is for Me

You should not be worried baby
Because my beauty is my beauty
I will not be scared
I will not be objectified
I will not let you walk on me

Because I am beauty
And beauty is me

Written at the New Utrecht High School workshop, Brooklyn, NY, May 7, 2019. A response to "How Do You Authenticate a Person," by Leroy J., who wrote at the Poets of Course workshop in Manhattan, NY, as a loose response to #100hardtruths #65: #fakenews #realtalk about black girls' liberation, by Cheryl Dunye, as well as #100hardtruths #52: Address fears about beauty, disability and aging, by Petra Kuppers.

PRACTICE STRATEGIC CONTEMPLATION

by Maro Perez and Lisa Moren

#100hardtruths #16: Practice strategic contemplation

A poetry writing script for a two-hour walk to generate a poem

1. Create a list of activities (with an alarm) to go off every 5 minutes for 2 hours
2. Go for a walk
3. Observe the truth of your surroundings
4. Allow for associations that relate to your observations and record during or after walk
5. If vibrations occur, then answer phone and follow your own prompt
6. Forget associations
7. Repeat until two hours are up

Written at the Ammerman Center workshop, New London, CT, Feb. 15, 2018. #100hardtruths #16 refers to ideas discussed in "Cámara Retórica: A Feminist Filmmaking Methodology for Rhetoric and Composition" by Alexandra Hidalgo. We Need Gentle Truths For Now *episode 14 engages Hidalgo and others about this productive algorithm.*

Experimental Escape Routes Needed: One Block

by Joseph Entin

#100hardtruths #22: Experimental escape routes needed

Muriel Rukeyser tells us: "Poetry can extend the document."
How does one document a neighborhood? What kind of poetics are required?
Neighborhoods occur at different scales:
The house, the stoop, the street, the quarter.
Where I live, life is block by block.
The block is a container
The block is a party
The block is a conflict
The block is a city
The block is an outrage
The block is a safehouse
The block is a trap
The block is being undone
The block is being rebuilt
The block is mine
The block is theirs
The block is filthy
The block is a history
The block is this tree, this stone, this door, this flag, this poem.

Written at the DOC@BC workshop, in Brooklyn, NY, Feb. 22, 2019. Based on #100hardtruths #92: Our oral histories, our oral stories are our truth, written by Faye Ginsburg about the work of Indigenous filmmaker, Amanda Strong, and also #100hardtruths #22, which was based on the program Disruptive Film, programmed by Sherry Millner and Ernest Larsen at Anthology Film Archives. Entin also produced a video-poem with the same name.

The Beauty of Weirdos, Your Human Hope

by Alexandra Juhasz

#100hardtruths #23: Galvanize people at the crossroads of cinema and community

Made at the Toronto workshop, Toronto, Ontario, March 17, 2018. This is the title and subject of the final We Need Gentle Truths For Now, *episode 18.*

It is not immaterialized it is lost

Group poem

#100hardtruths #27: New image holding environments needed

ALL I WANT
TO BE

I DO NOT NEED 1000
FOLLOWERS I JUST
NEED MY MOM

Loss when it is not
there, loss when
it is there.

The irony in having

A body now

Written at the Devil's Dyke workshop, Brighton, England, March 19, 2018. #100hardtruths #27 is based upon Alexandra Juhasz's review of the International Center of Photography exhibition, Perpetual Revolution: The Image and Social Change.

Battle for the Truth

by Mya Rigoli

#100hardtruths #29: Interrupt the narrative

the internet is a machine of complacency
my neck a battleground for the hands of the foolish
i want to choke on the words
that do not belong to me
i want to spit back the fake news like
crumpled cash in a coin machine
interrupt the narrative
like every are we there yet
from the backseat of mama's car
when google maps didn't call my mouth a home
know my address like every
where am i?
can be answered in
a number
a value
the amount of followers on an instagram page
i want to click refresh on our history
and know that I would be proud
of every trip that i've made
i want to know the footprints i follow
once belonged to a beating heart
that the truth bleeds the same color
as a bit tongue and stained teeth
the riot cannot be seen when the battleground
has been closed to the public
when our history will soon be closed to the public

Written at the Get Lit workshop, Los Angeles, CA, Oct. 13, 2018. #100hardtruths #29 refers to "10 Ways to Be a Feminist Media Activist," by Feminist Frequency.

Not Flat Enough

Group poem

#100hardtruths #37: Size matters; we have to be minimalist

it has to be
autonomous

me as productivity machine
programmed by my phone
input+data+body = product (ivity)

The space between
Liberation and entrapment

Written at the Devil's Dyke workshop, Brighton, England, March 19, 2018. #100hardtruths #37 refers to the words of filmmaker Agnes Varda: "We have to be minimalist. A small event, if we can understand it, reconciles us a little bit with the world."

Now it's the receding horizon of possibility

Anonymous poetry fragment

#100hardtruths #40: Challenge the narrative of (African) American progress

Now it's the
receding
horizon of
possibility
It is a strange impossibility that
Is true that
We have to work with
Black-lives-matter
As a proposition not
A reality.

Written at the Toronto workshop, Toronto, Ontario, March 17, 2018. #100hardtruths #40 refers to the exhibition Library of Black Lies *by Edgar Arceneaux.*

"there there, it's so much worse than that, so much worse" A poetry writing algorithm

by Lucas Crane

#100hardtruths #49: Support cinematic solidarity against Islamophobia

>respond to any "I'm trying to..." sentence with "there there, it's so much worse than that, so much worse," then say why.

Written at the Ammerman Center workshop, New London, CT, Feb. 15, 2018. #100hardtruths #49 refers to an effort by the Seventh Art Stand "to elevate the cinemas and stories" of people from the countries affected by President Donald Trump's travel ban: Iran, Iraq, Libya, Somalia, Sudan, Syria, and Yemen.

the go fund mes never end

by Alex Rafaelov

#100hardtruths #74: Stay open to contradictions and power #offline

Most of my friends are drug addicts and alcoholics,
They kill them selves over and over again
They say waking up every day is their worst nightmare
But they wake up anyway
I've never seen anyone more happy or alive then them
They all have pretty pictures of them selves up on their Instagram but talk about how much they want to die on their finstas
They have the best laughs and the warmest smiles
I see myself in them
They probably see themselves in me
We see ourselves in each other as a way to make us whole
Anis father killed him self a couple months back
cancer tucked jesses mom into bed at night then forgot to wake her up
Lillies mom died when she was little and she was left with
her father who used to touch her
I still don't know the whole story
Xavis dad beats her
And we all know someone who's killed them self or a friend who died
I saw how Dina killed herself when I was 13
I've been playing hide and seek with my emotions ever since
The blood didn't splatter
And there was no Big Bang as the train split through her neck
At that point you couldn't tell what was throat and what was neck everything was inside out
Just like this life that I'm living
The memory's I have are made out of nightmares
I wish they were nightmares
I don't want it to be real
I talk about my traumas on my finsta account hope to turn these memories into stories
We all sit around the pit fire that is the internet and exchange ghost stories of our past
Hope to turn these pleas for help into prayers and then into miracles
I've been linking too many go fundmes to my instagram account
All the money in the world and there still isn't enough to pay the funeral costs
I've been reposting pictures of missing children who wandered off to the moon and never came back
I hope they
Come back
And if not

I hope they land somewhere amongst the stars
We drink and drink and drink like coke and rum came from the fountain of youth
We don't feel real
When the world is dancing beneath your feet and your head is too fucked up to notice the difference between dirt and the sky anything feels real
People say they get fucked up to escape reality but we lost reality's definition long ago
We know nothing about it
Everything seems like reality now even when it isn't
Even when I'm disassociated from life
It doesn't feel like the world isn't there it feels like I'm not there like
Like I'm the one who's not real
It's normal for me to not feel real
That place in limbo is almost like my second home
I was scrolling through my twitter feed the other day and every other post is
A political hoax or a missing kid
Sometimes I want to believe the government is some giant allusion made to scare us like the boogie man
Sometimes I wanna believe all those kids ran away and came back home after a day or too
But go fund mes never end
And we just keep adding up the funeral costs
We share our grief and condolences in the comments section and virtually tell the world things will get better
But at the end of the day
I go home to empty bottles of wine and empty some more just to pass the time
I go home and wonder if I'm really alive
I'm lying in my bed wondering if maybe I just really wanna die
My phone goes off again
It's a twitter post notification from god
He said "@alex You're already dead"
Sent from my iPhone

Written at the Get Lit workshop, Los Angeles, CA, Oct. 13, 2018.

Explaining Myself

by Irene Villaseñor

#100hardtruths #85: Make productive fake documentaries

I.
Falling asleep while reading the Joy Luck Club (1989)
During breaks from IQ testing in elementary school
Must mean I'm one overworked Asian kid
But the truth is that book bored me — and I'll fast forward
throughout its movie adaptation too. Mishima
was way more exciting because I'd rather be
a Sailor Who Fell from Grace with the Sea than Waverly Jong.

II.
I don't know how I'm supposed to interpret compliments
That I'm beautiful like Mulan, especially when it's coming from
sweet elderly Chinese women — like my acupuncturist. Am I
pretty like Disney's *Mulan* (1998) or historical Hua Mulan?
Bridal Mulan or Warrior Mulan? Do they really think the only
striking reference I'll have of an attractive or powerful Asian
woman is a cartoon? Or are they assuming I'd be familiar with
ancient Chinese poetry due to my studies? I will never know.

III.
Nutshelling Battle Hymn of a Tiger Mother (2011) means pointing
out Chinese people in the Philippines circled their wagons and
defended themselves by pursuing excellence as their main protection
in hostile environments. But ended up eating their young in the
process. And some people keep spreading this disease.

IV.
Crazy Rich Asians (2018) may just upgrade old Asian stereotypes and
introduce new ones. Already there's disapproval for a casting as a leading
man Henry Golding, who's half-white. But his other half is Iban from Borneo.
That part of his heritage comes to the fore because I'm not looking for
whiteness. But seeking instances where being indigenous isn't shameful,
ugly, remote, brokeass, or backward buffoonery. If more Asians could see
and value indigeneity, then maybe whiteness would be less important.

Written at the Race in the Media workshop, Brooklyn, NY, May 5, 2018.

Our oral stories are our truth

by L. Dominguez

#100hardtruths #86: Resist how we are framed

I felt I was in the moment of silence because I was shy, a little bit social
and my identity has been changing for the better and worst of me.

I was never rejected not because I have a disability,
I just didn't want to talk to people in high school.
because I was shy, and anti-social and I wanted to be by myself.

I have a story to tell about myself and my surroundings,
I keep it real about myself as a human being
and I have many things to control myself and not to worry
what other people think of me.

Written at the Poets of Course Workshop, Manhattan, NY, Oct. 2, 2018, as a response to #100hardtruths #92: Our oral histories, our oral stories are our truth, and to #100hardtruths #86: Resist how we are framed, by queer historian and writer, Hugh Ryan.

I hold the phone in my hand

by Sam Solomon

#100hardtruths #94: Always look for the real thing

I hold the phone in my hand. My hand is freezing. I look at the phone. I look away from the phone. There's a world there.
The phone says that's a lie. The world is in the phone. I face the phone and tap. I flip from phone to face. You face the phone and walk away. Phone, get in the sea.
We're doing this for everyone. You're everyone else. Come on, come out.
Aerobicize with me. It isn't for me, I promise. I promise I'm more than me.
It's for the thing we're not yet. It's true I haven't missed you. It's also true I have.

Written at the University of Sussex workshop, Falmer, England, March 19, 2018. #100hardtruths #94 was written by curator, Danielle Jackson. Solomon read his poem in conversation with the work of the students at New Utrecht High in Brooklyn and my adult child and their partner in the first episode of We Need Gentle Truths For Now, *"The Real Internet is a Fake."*

We Flatten. Human Touch

Group poem

#100hardtruths #97: Digital participation is reflexive

Being together,
Feeling, acknowledging
And letting it go.
I REFLECT
SOMETHING
BODIES RECEIVING

Written collectively at the Devil's Dyke workshop, Brighton, England, March 19, 2018.

A Picture that Will Never Tell My Story

by Ash and Ty

#100hardtruths #99: Information overload needs positive feedback effects

T| If you don't have a profile picture
You don't have no character
Even just black says something

A| People can be secretive

T| Secretive isn't the word
They're more to themselves

A| Oh, independent then
You having a black screen makes
you not want to talk to someone

T| Just being plain

A| It's more than one reason
They don't want to be social
They don't want to make friends

T| There's a difference between knowing your life
And someone actually knowing

A| Yeah! — but you don't know —
I would have no friends and
you would never know

Written at the New Utrecht High School workshop, Brooklyn, NY, May 7, 2019, in response to the poem "A picture that will never tell my story," by Aodhan Gallagher, written at the New York University workshop and based loosely on #100hardtruths #69: Ghosts can't tell stories, by curator Quito Zeigler. #100hardtruths #99 responds to the writing of Tiziana Terranova. We Need Gentle Truths For Now *episode 15, "Ghosts Can't Tell Stories," featuring scholars Jih-Fei Cheng and Nishant Shahani, extends this line of thinking by connecting it to the ongoing distribution of the AIDS crises and the poetry of Ross Gay.*

our internet truths trump media lies

we must name, share, and honor our own lived experiences within social media

as another form of honesty in desperate times.

Let's first do this offline, together where we live, work, struggle or learn

An egg speaks
fed on Thich Nhat Hahn, Joy Harjo, and FemTechNet

by Jacque Wernimont

#100hardtruths #53: Tame and disarm dangerous algorithms

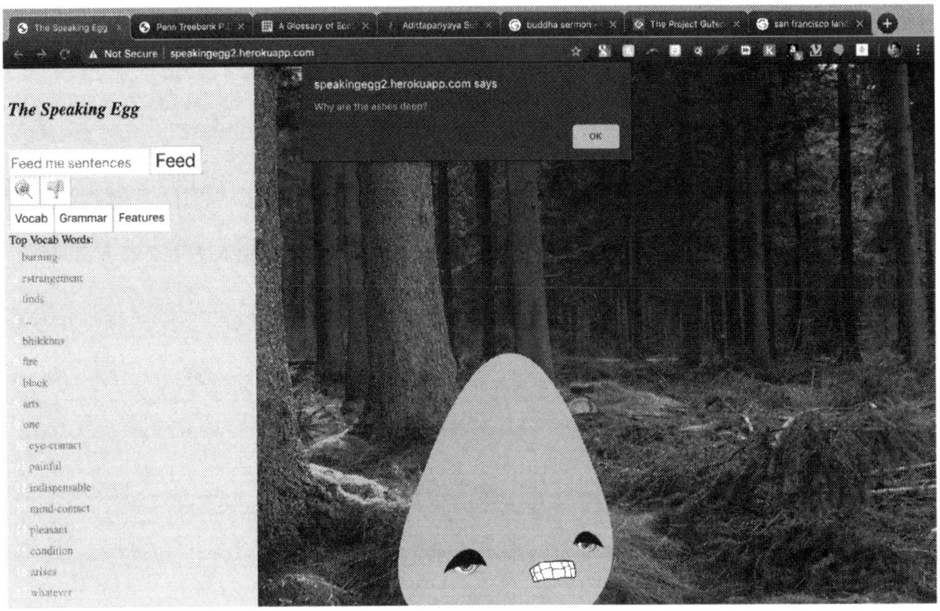

Voice is perfect
RESOLVE is now conflict, (and)
Disappearance is peace.
(With the) demise of content (and) fellow others
We realized X. But dark means archive (and)
Someone continues reduced.
Image time well,
identities abandoning
Analysis of clouds; we will survive our history
Internet is surface (and) morning remembers.

Written at the Dartmouth College workshop, Hanover, NH, Feb. 25, 2019. #100hardtruths #53 was contributed by Geert Lovink from his "Overcoming the Disillusioned Internet: On the Principles of Meme Design." Jacque, the egg, and Geert sing and read in We Need Gentle Truths For Now *episode 8, "Tame and Disarm Dangerous Algorithms."*

My Body is real; what is the feminist way to survive

Anonymous Fragment Triplet

#100hardtruths #12: We need things to help us get closer to the truth

MY BODY is real
has a history
holds knowledge
creates
understandings justice
lives complexity
can heal
changes
deserves life
transforms reality
....
What is the feminist
way to survive?
....
flexible
claim
making

Written at the Toronto workshop, Toronto, Ontario, March 17, 2018. #100hardtruths #12 refers to the writing of Mike Caufield's online book Web Literacy for Student Fact-Checkers.

hurt stress

Group poem

#100hardtruths #18: A cultural change about how we make sense of information required

A poem created by participants reading words, in a circle, for their thoughts and responses to fake news and... a feeling, a technology, a feeling, and a site where they experience these on their bodies.

Hurt stress
Clammy
Socialize
Psychotic stress
Overwhelmed addicted planet.
Cellphone, phone, cellphone plug.
Cellphone, ipod, email, iphone, cellphone.
Phone.

Robotic rich blurriness.
Connections
Expansive failure.
Distracted attacked
Another life.

Brain heart eyes mind
Stomach neck
Above my eyes
Brain
Mind.

Performed at the LaGuardia Community College workshop, Queens, NY, April 24, 2018.

Government Lies Now

by Michael G.

#100hardtruths #31: Look deeper into the migrant experience

Government always lies to people in America.
Because it always Trump
as the TV and YouTube.
Such a fool
I want a turn a real truth
Some Americans us white trash people
don't like Mexicans or others
they not right to doing it.

Written at the second Poets of Course Workshop, Manhattan, NY, in Jan. 2019. #100hardtruths #31 focuses on an art show, State of Exception/Estado de Excepción, which "presents traces of the human experience — objects left behind in the desert by undocumented migrants on their journey into the U.S. and other forms of data," collected as part of the research of University of Michigan anthropologist Jason De León's Undocumented Migration project. De León reads and responds to this poem, in conversation with Mike G., in We Need Gentle Truths For Now *episode 2, "Look Deeper Into the Migrant Experience."*

do not be distracted from the truth

by M. Astley

#100hardtruths #34: Place matters/re-flecting the border

do not be distracted from the truth
that you make with your own body
Solidity is a useful illusion
It gets us through the day
solidity (gets us) resists us
tectonic assurance is fragile ground
the truth is the emptiness in the middle of the atom
the truth is the impressionability of matter, of us,
the truth is the space we fight to shape

Written at the University of Sussex workshop, Falmer, England, March 19, 2018. #100hardtruths #34 refers to an art intervention of the same name by ERRE and Margarita Garcia Asperas, "Re/flecting the Border," 2017. Astley reads this poem in conversation with Natalie Bookchin, in We Need Gentle Truths For Now *episode 10, "Silicon Valley's Entrepreneurial Capitalism Leaves Rubble in its Wake."*

Black Lives Matter

by Gerard G.

#100hardtruths #44: Black Lives Matter

Black people die every year from drugs,
violence and AIDS.
Black people die every year from police choke holds and death row.
like that gots to go
Sometimes racist Trump says black never lives matter
because Martin Luther King Jr, Malcolm X, needs to have their pockets fatter.
It's always time to stop all the racist jokes
'cause in the real world black people ain't B's noting no coax.
It can be B.I.G, POC, Jam Master Jay
can live forever
but they will never die in my heart
'cause it's a place to start.
When it's time for the black Revolution to start the war
it's time for them to take it far.
Sometimes Aunt Jemima, Uncle Ben keep saving the coons for food
but black lives matter is still in the mood.
'Cause if I was in the mood for love
like God is still up above
I might as well fly high like a dove.
Between blacks black folks always beefing with white folks in different states
I'm all around them in every day
don't mean I change my way.

Written at the second Poets of Course workshop, Manhattan, NY, 2018. This was transformed into a video-poem of the same name at their third workshop. It is also the subject of We Need Gentle Truths For Now *episode 7, "Black Lives Matter: A Cultural Change about How We Makes Sense of Information Required," in which Gerard and his mother have "the talk" about his safety as a Black disabled man in New York City.*

Our oral stories are our truth

by Mike G.

#100hardtruths #52: Address fears about beauty, disability and aging

my stories in my life is disabled
because I lost my hearings and low vision
not able to see
but I could see very hard.

I felt some way
I do my family treat right
I got older in 90s to 2000s
many people do not treat me bad
I told Jesus that help bad people's pain.

I identify myself to be proud
I do things and try real and have kids of my own.
I wish has cure to fix me and other disabled people
it the truth.
also I don't like people to hurt my feelings.

Written at the Poets of Course workshop, Manhattan, NY, Oct. 2, 2018. It refers to #100hardtruths #92: Our oral histories, our oral stories are our truth, written by Faye Ginsburg, which refers to the work of Indigenous artist Amanda Strong, and to #100hardtruths #52, written by disability theorist and artist Petra Kuppers.

Questions?

Anonymous poetry fragment

#100hardtruths #54: #100questions to resist against future Presidents, even if we like them

where did social media come from?
what are you a fan of?
who is similar to you who is
different from you?
why is fake news pleasurable?
who is your favorite person on
the internet?
which website do you visit the
most? who owns it?
how can technology make magic

Written at the Toronto workshop, Toronto, Ontario, March 17, 2018. #100hardtruths #54 was contributed by AIDS activist and organizer, Theodore Kerr.

how do we best make fun of power?

Anonymous triplet of fragments

#100hardtruths #56: Subversion through grinning; learn truths from radical Black artists who lived through civil rights

How do we best
make fun of power?
....
radical
change
cannot
come from
isolation;
it must be
collaborative
....
time
+
repetition
+
stamina
in material

Written at the Toronto workshop, Toronto, Ontario, March 17, 2018.
#100hardtruths #56 was contributed by filmmaker, Stephen Winter.

I'm a veteran and a refugee

Group script-poem produced at HASTAC by responding over two sessions to a meme, and a poem, and some feelings, and technologies by Anne Balsamo, Alexandra Juhasz, Gary Lai, Nicole Manson, Tara McPherson, Roopa Vasudevan, Aneesh Vashisht, Michele White

#100hardtruths #58: Choose to know, name, and share your internet truths (an invitation)

I'm a veteran.

I'm a refugee.

I'm a veteran and a refugee.

I'm a veteran refugee. I always leave home every chance I get because home is not enough to satisfy everything you need. So, you go other places. And I've never felt at home anywhere because I was always on the move looking for the next place to go. On the other hand, I've always been at home wherever I've been.

Does anybody like that story? Does anyone here feel like that story resonates for you? Can you join us?

Yes. That resonates because I moved a lot when I was growing up and so I don't have one place that's really home except where I make home with people I love.

After hurricane Katrina there was no food or water in New Orleans. Cuba offered to come and provide us with water. The US said no.

I feel terrible that that happened to you. I feel awful. That means that you didn't have enough resources when you could've had some.

Everywhere I walk into, I walk in with my identity as a First Nations woman. Everywhere I go

that's how I identify. Yes, I've been mistaken for a Mexican or Polynesian when I've been in those places or even in Southern California I was mistaken as Mexican. But I went to Africa for the first time with my daughter cause she's half Kenyan and I was told I wasn't Indigenous; in fact I was white. To everybody there because my skin wasn't Black, I was white, and actually, on a drive I got referred to, cause my daughter's stepmom was driving us, the police officer asked, "oh are you taking the boss around?"

That story resonates with me because I was born and grew up in the U.S., and I have traveled around a lot of places in the world and I'm never identified as an American. I'm always identified as something else. "Where are you really from?" And, in the moments that I go back to India, I am always not identified as an Indian because I carry myself in such a Western way that I couldn't possibly be from there.

Written at the HASTAC workshop, Vancouver, British Columbia, May 18, 2019.

Resist how we are framed

Exquisite corpse poem

#100hardtruths #61: Connect voting rights, disability and the marketplace of services

thoughts
are from the mind
We believe no one should have to face a mental health problem
alone
Feel lonely as I seek truth
truth

Written at the DIGITAL EngAGEmentConference, Manhattan, NY, May 18, 2018. #100hardtruths #61 was written by media theorist Anne Balsamo, about her sister, Laura. We Need Gentle Truths For Now *episode 16 extends this conversation by thinking about the poetry of Adrienne Rich, David Wojnarowicz, and Audre Lorde (as read by my children and my partner's child), as first introduced to the project by Hugh Ryan, in #100hardtruths #86: Resist how we are framed.*

Don't Look

by Kiy Gentle

#100hardtruths #62: Don't look

Shhhhh
can you hear that
I think you've made them angry
Shhhhh
Don't look, they're watching us
Wanting us to keep believing
I heard a survivor type once that skepticism is just a side affect of reality
But then again
I haven't heard from her lately
Let's just keep going
Stopping is a place of growth
And when they feel they are getting small
They teach us new ways to survive

Written at the Get Lit workshop, Los Angeles, CA, Oct. 13, 2018.

Ghosts can't tell stories

by Gracie Thorne

#100hardtruths #69: Ghosts can't tell stories

I
Now search the deceased
in your omniscient search box;
grieve your lost likes.

II
Sad face the obituary.
Now you can miss the funeral.
Check for updates.

III
Timehop memory,
because ghosts can't tell stories,
but do keep thumb prints.

IV
Do continue stalking
the bereavement of a group
known as a friends list.

V
You really are helping
by poking them into posting
painful pictures.

VI
Post how you knew them,
because ghosts can't tell stories.
but you can send hearts.

VII
Click right and 'see friendship.'
Share your brief interactions
to archive your grief.

VIII
Keep looking for grief.
Retweet deep quotes on death.
Follow the close family.

IX
Thank your tired thumbs,
because ghosts can't tell stories.
But they are online.

Written at the University of Sussex workshop, Falmer, England, March 19, 2018.
#100hardtruths #69 was written by curator and organizer, Quito Zeigler.

Historical Context Depending

Anonymous poetry fragment couplet

#100hardtruths #72: Learn how to see Palestine

Historical
Context
Depending
....
Imagining
other points
of reference
we might share

Written at the Toronto workshop, Toronto, Ontario, March 17, 2018. #100hardtruths #72 was written by visual cultural scholar and activist, Nick Mirzoeff.

Our oral stories are our truth

by Maria Z.

#100hardtruths #92: Our oral histories, our oral stories are our truth

Our oral stories, begins October 5th 2018. I was in front of house which is the dining room at Shake Shack I was in uniform then at 3:15 in the afternoon when Marisol and Kristen began blinking the lights and called us into the kitchen and I did not know what was going on then Kristen announced that I made employee of the month. And I almost cried in front of my team members. I felt very shocked and happy the next day Ronnie came in and was shocked. When I got home around 6:30 in the evening and waited for company to leave I told my mom I made employee of the month my mom almost cried and fainted at the news.

Written at the Poets of Course workshop, Manhattan, NY, Oct. 2, 2018. #100hardtruths #92 was written by media anthropologist Faye Ginsburg, featuring the work of Indigenous video artist Amanda Strong.

Conclusion: How to Have a Fake News Poetry Workshop

This book offers things to do with others as well as things that were done before and for you. It proffers that making and making use of poetry, with people known to us, can create verification engines that rely on and benefit from belief structures outside the endangering logics of the internet and the fake news that it and we propagate. Given the personally felt and materially actualized violence, distrust, and anxiety engendered by the escalating failings of internet culture most generally, and social media more specifically, the book shares Fake News Poetry Workshops (and their results) as methods (and their things) to help us better understand, while also countering and improving our contemporary media state.

The things that workshops offer are small, slow, and careful. The things we can do are also small: reading, writing, sharing, listening, and learning. Workshops are explicitly against logics of scaling up; they are local and curated. They are unlike the vast internet and all its holdings and tabulations. They are against while also about the internet and its foundations in fakery. The actions proposed and modeled are set within different and explicit belief structures, with clear intended purposes and outcomes, part of which is doing and being in a place and time defined and experienced by a small group of participants. Against, in opposition to, and contrasting what it also hopes to better understand — contra-the-internet — I ask you to think about fake news using poetry so as to slow down and use your time to do what the internet hopes to paper over: caring for things, and those who made them, by attending to their and our own place and time.

The things are poems; the doing is writing, reading, listening, being, staging, caring, and learning together in our own honored places and times. Others already involved in the project and process have written and shared smart, careful, useful, moving things — art — about fake news as poetry for you to learn and feel from.

This project is as small, and local, as friendship, learning, and human connection. The depth of that continues to move me and stays complicated as well as central: to know and to be with people to create the internet and the world we want.

The internet holds much of value and a lot of trash. The shared project of art-making intensifies and saturates these already meaningful relationships, leaving poems and art as traces of our live, embodied engagements about the all-too-deadening internet. And then there are photos and videos, performances, and songs. And also, finally, this writing, where I try to testify to and also depict on paper the power of collective activities that begin with a crucial and shared goal and are based in thought and art. Our grounding is in place and also in ideas.

There are impressive, demanding, and useful schools of theory and practice, built over decades or centuries, about media literacy, fakes, social media, and more. While these foundational concepts refer to rigorous and complex traditions, they point to understandable things. The internet is owned, managed, designed, and monetized by governments and corporations who hide this truth in plain sight while telling us something else: that it is for public and personal expression and democratic unfoldings. We know better but participate anyway. Part of this shared deception is rooted in these owners', and we users', increasing interest in simple-to-use, ready-made, quick, slick templates and customs that enable and simplify expression, as well as its distribution and consumption. Our embrace of these technologies counters centuries of other thoughtful holdings: our commitments to other structures that allow for human expression to form within time, dense shapes, and systems of rhetoric outside of easy aphorisms, juridical or journalistic rule, or mechanical or mathematical logic. There is nothing inherently wrong with our newer systems — short and sweet, quick and strong — unless these tactics are taken up and consolidated by forces of patriarchal, corporate, or violent power or for uses that weaponize their strengths at consolidation and intensity.

Capital and patriarchy structure the internet as they do the world. Online this takes the confusing and stimulating shape of dissembled and reassembled binaries — interlocked and never fully clear — such as true/false or fake/real. In our once pure, non-digital world, these binaries were more straightforwardly delineated, or at least pretended to be, structuring rather neatly many of our shared experiences, businesses, and governments, as well as our perceptions and understandings of them. But on the internet a different arrangement has been introduced: a muddle of binaries. This is odd because, of course, the internet (unlike the world) is built of 0s and 1s. Binary. But in my early work on YouTube, I came to understand, along with my students and fellow YouTubers, that for YouTube and other social media, an underlying sense of disbelief, lack of clarity, or irony prevails. At first, this lack of solid ground (is this true or fake? who owns this place? was this made by people, bots, or corporations? is this public or private?) was understood as kinda-sorta pleasurable, smart, or even mostly true. A formative, buzzy, wise-ass uncertainty dominated our experiences, barely papered over by a competing system: a design and architecture mimicking coherence and simplicity. Everywhere across these superficial and facile surfaces, we were informed that we would have a voice. That it would be fun and easy. That it was free. Even in the first years, we probably knew better. But still we engaged brightly, eagerly, and in amazing numbers (as we still do, in greater numbers, if less brightly): taking advantage of a definitive set of lies that we all bought into together.

Visible manifestations of phony coherence created by free, slick, and user-friendly platforms distract our attention from something else we know to be true but that remains harder to see; the internet's governmental backbone and corporate architecture, ownership, and value(s). The foundational lies of today's internet — that it is a public good rather than a monetized commodity; that it promotes or is even interested in freedom of expression and civil discourse; that our actions there are activism or social rather than mere consumerism (of ourselves and things) — are camouflaged by facetious platitudes about the norms and values of this place that most of us more and more frequently call home.

Rooted in other's greed, power, abuse, and deception, our internet actions and interactions are often deceptively justified, and felt, as calls to freedom of expression, consumption, and interaction. While there's nothing wrong with any of these qualities per se, especially as or about entertainment, their digital articulations are simply and truly not the best forums to sustain and promote education and other civic needs. We have learned the hard way that social media logics and platforms are not equipped to support reliable news and elections, or healthy democracies or civil societies.

Experimental bodies of art making, and the theories and communities that surround and sustain them, challenge us to contemplate how media and state truths are made and how to disrupt these processes by taking up other systems of seeing, showing, and knowing. Experimental representational strategies help us to see differently. The press of the imagination alongside the image, the aesthetic amidst the indexical, the affective within the factual, can render contemplative states that allow us to see other structures. We need other ways to look because speed and contextlessness are built into socially mediated images themselves, not just where they sit or how they move. However, as I consider in #100hardtruths #27, "good image-holding environments" can also help by producing context, building history, analysis, and frames for the flow of evidence that include access to the humans who have lived, witnessed, or embody the experience being evidenced. Perhaps counterintuitively, a poetic approach to these experiences can itself be such a holding environment, offering our fragments frameworks from the imagination, the aesthetic, the intellectual, or the affective.

And then, there's a related need for new ways to imagine practices of looking. We are in sore need of ethical prep work for our reception of evidence not just through the creation of more context, but commitments of more time for our engagements. In an era when the speed and volume of image production and consumption equates tragically to the speed of image forgetting, as well as a linked sense that there might be nothing to do in the face of the endless violent tragedies that such images record, giving our time to build structures that hold viral images, and taking time to frame our viewing of them, can be steps toward an ethical project of witnessing.

Virality is also a precondition for fake news, a crisis none of us view as right or true (by definition!). This contradiction underwrites our current crisis. #fakenews, unlike real news, reveals the logic and cycles of virality, a mad explosion of attention that flattens and simplifies whatever is under scrutiny by having to bear, while needing to use, the weight of mass attention and production. When ideas move fast in their production, reception, or spread, we give up the time necessary for research, verification, contemplation, and action. Ideas that are well liked and massively shared depend upon simplicity, consolidation, or generic acceptability. For this we readily give up subtlety, complexity, and depth. All the deeper work that also occurs is harder to see given the clamor and the clutter. Exhaustion, a gutting of integrity, and a quick hard move to deception, irony, and play follow. Given its definitive cycle, virality is good for many things: branding, selling, fun, and power. However, virality is not effective for social justice, reasoned expression, compassion, or change, where depth, connection, careful consideration, and context matter more than do brief recognition, superficial attention, or momentary if strong emotion.

Then, with the pairing of our previous president and this social media, we witnessed how the rules of sexism, networked technologies, pursuit of approval, and state violence perfectly align. This definitive mix of internet-fueled numbers, masculine grandiosity, and real-world hostility is what I mean by this project's core adage, "virality is virility." Nuclear threats or racist tweets enact a macho posturing central to political personae and operations — virility — rooted in sanctioned if often despicable forms of male aggression.

The reasons to counter fake news are self-evident. Harder to fathom, given these conditions: *how* might we outlast virility and its virile harms? We need systems that foreground ethical care, time, and reasoned consideration between how we live and how we express, share, and know. Feminist and queer affect theory proposes one method to register these many connections and discrepancies. Affect is how the body speaks, knows, and communicates alongside the rational, the semiotic, the legal. Each body, in its lived spaces and encounters with the world, outside or alongside the merely cognitive, experiences related methods of knowing and being that are felt internally while also often shown and showable to the self and others.

We now inhabit a new home for our expression and much of it works: we have access to more people, knowledge, art, and connections than any human could enjoy in a lifetime, no matter how fast we move and use it. But the internet is also a sorry substitute for the building of engaged, place-based interactions that sustain people, movements, and ideas. In fact, I have called this — the production, movement, and connecting to and through digital words and images — proto-political. That is, all this digital sharing, learning, speaking, and imaging can be exciting steps toward more informed well-being and world-changing. However, the more we live and love and work there, given its corporate hosts and the deceptions we sign off on to keep us there, the more we agree to a partial-life in systems of representation that can only point to our greater possibility. There is real potential nascent within and written into our words and images, as well as their reception. Each digital gesture registers what we could render in our bodies and our world.

Online, alone, together, we acknowledge to ourselves that we are here, and that we can be momentarily heard and seen, if not yet in the ways that feel most human or that might be most productive for change. To be more human again, to do what humans do best — strive for change; live with complexity; be with each other — we'll need to refind and reinvent embodied, situated, representational projects. As quoted by Hugh Ryan in his #100hardtruths #86: Resist how we are framed, Audre Lorde wrote in *Learning from the Sixties,* "Within each one of us there is some piece of humanness that knows we are not being served by the machine which orchestrates crisis after crisis and is grinding all our futures into dust."

The internet is our condition, one of skepticism, bounty, expression, art, corporate control, and structuring falsities. The internet is our condition of violence, our condition of power, and a place of resistance. It and we aren't going anywhere... yet. Lorde also said, "We know what it is to be lied to, and we know how important it is not to lie to ourselves." Our words and communities and art can and must be the sites where we distill our human clarity, in all its rioting complexity. This painful and hard work needs communities of care and practice to hold it, not internet towers of any strength or shape. For I am not a machine, nor a tyrant, a corporation, a nation-state, someone's data, or something's product. Nor are you. We are people, and we want and need more than the successful transmission of messages and data. We want connection, goodness, honesty, reason, feeling, and change. Yes to sitting together in the noise, being together in the clarifying beauty and intensity of our shared humanity and profound human production. I accept that I am complicit and accountable for my role therein. I would like to learn how to not participate, and instead collaborate toward change.

I tried something else and invite you to as well: Fake News Poetry Workshops. The key product is the radical pedagogy. The poetry is the excuse and an opportunity, a better way to be smart, ethical, true, and heard in this time of fake news and social media. Poetry allows us to communicate with and reflect upon each other outside of the structures and vernaculars, which, in the name of rationality, proof, truth, and power, are producing our current chaotic, disturbing, and often fake digital reality. In and with poetry, our energy can be focused not on quantifiable outcomes but on the creation of an atmosphere of authenticity, safety, and dialogue; on the making of place; and on the creation of meaning. Fake News Poetry Workshops participate in an anti-meme flow that slows, stops, restarts, listens, honors, and makes anew again.

So, be a poet. Host a Fake News Poetry Workshop in your own community and find some friends or colleagues to do so with you! Here are twenty steps, drawn from the wisdom of previous poets and participants, that are procedural, conceptual, and also motivational.

Fake News Poetry Workshops in 20 Steps

1) **Create a team.** A poet or a teacher or a student or an engaged citizen form a group and agree to collaborate to create and lead a Fake News Poetry Workshop. For the twenty workshops I led from February 15, 2018 to July 2019, this team-building was a loose if magnetic process of affiliation. Sometimes I approached a poet or a teacher; some poets found me through my travels or their relations to other participants. For the first workshop, I found, through some poet friends, and subsequently reached out to poet-collaborator Kyle Booten because his scholarly and artistic work is organized around machine learning, technological platforms, and poetry. I sent him an email, we had several conversations, and we finally met for the first time IRL when we lead the first workshop in New London, Connecticut.

> When Alex Juhasz asked me to help lead a workshop on the relationship between poetry and fake news, I felt intrigued but uncertain. After all, so many of the proposed antidotes

to mendacious digital media come from the technological and ideological milieu of digital media itself: if certain accounts (be they humans or bots) spread lies on social networks, we need the networks to identify and disable them.

— Kyle Booten, "10 Tries, 100 Poems (Take 1): 'Psychotechnologies of Care, Algorithms of Attention,'" March 21, 2018.

2) **Agree to learn and teach together in a community.** Workshop leaders should believe they have something to learn: from each other and, even more, once their community joins in.

The aim of Get Lit/Words Ignite is to develop the voice of youth poets. We use poetry to increase literacy, empower youth, and inspire communities. ... It is a beautiful thing to watch talented youth poets be inspired by other poets to share their stories, to observe the process of great art in conversation with one another.

— Kelly Grace Thomas, "10 Tries, 100 Poems (Take 2): 'Poetry is the New Watchdog,'" March 11, 2018.

3) **Begin in a place and make it your own.**

The poets focused some of the dialogue around the Get Lit organization's physical space being a community space, comparing it to digital community space. Notions of authentic relationships and safe spaces came to the forefront of the discussion. In their dialogue, the poets were taking part in active place-making: agreeing, riffing, and questioning internet communities and the digital information age in real time, fully present with one another. This activity primed the meaning-creation of their writing and performance.

— Aneesah Ettress and Xiomara Rodriguez, "10 Tries, 100 Poems (Take 3): 'The Poetics of Place-Making,'" April 7, 2018.

4) **Identify shared norms and/or interests between the collaborating teaching poet and her anticipated participants.** Each site and its participants are unique. Workshops can happen in cities, towns, colleges, community spaces, offices, or homes. Their timescapes can be equally unique: the highly scheduled meeting slot of a conference session; one meeting devoted to the task from a weekly commitment of an already extant group; at a party; during a strike. Each will be peopled by participants with different skills, bonds, and temperaments: high schoolers, professors, the cognitively disabled, the artistically refined, the naive at heart.

Alex arrived in Brighton during the seventh week of our term, and yet we had not met as a group for the previous three weeks. This was because I was on strike as a member of the University and Colleges Union over the proposed slashing of the pension scheme. ... Alex and I decided that the best approach to holding a workshop under these conditions was to spend our first hour-long session asking everyone in the room to address the following questions:

1) What is something about the past three weeks that you know to be true? How do you know this?

2) What is something you heard during the past three weeks that you know to be false? Where did you hear this and how do you know it's false?

—Sam Solomon, "10 Tries, 100 Poems (Take 4): 'Truth and Lies at the Intersection of Activism and Art,'" May 6, 2018.

5) **Plan your workshop.** There are as many approaches to a workshop as there are poets, communities, and places to hold them. Example: The Devil's Dyke workshop, held in Brighton, England, was organized by and for a collective of queer feminist poets to whom Sam Solomon had introduced me months before I came to England. (Sam came to me by way of my friend and colleague, Alisa Lebow, his colleague at University of Sussex.) Three members of the Devil's Dyke Network created a workshop focusing on the links between somatic and cyborg experiences.

Creative writing and media workshop with Alexandra Juhasz, Tuesday, March 20.

Aim: Explore our presence on social media and the contestation of fake/hegemonic news through creative means.

Check in. Ground ourselves in our feelings and express them. In a circle standing with everyone facing outwards: a). Think of a word that describes how you're feeling right now; b). Think about your body from toes up, to your head and out to your fingers. Try to make a movement that expresses the word you thought of. Practice it once for yourself and turn when you're ready; c). In a flowing round each presents their movement and says their word if they wish.

—Claudia Treacher, Linda Paoli, and Helen Dixon. From the workshop plan, "Creative Writing and Media Workshop with Alexandra Juhasz."

6) **Enjoy some back and forth.** The planning between instructors is itself a significant part of the radical digital media literacy. Be open to new ideas. We all have more to learn! I reached out to Barbara Browning quite early in the life of this project because she is a scholar from whom I have learned much. Her novels artfully comingle prose, poetry, email, real and imagined "characters," all depicting a series of close-to-real events that trouble the fake-real binary due to the mechanisms, norms, and desires that fan internet culture and communication. One conversation led to another, and she volunteered to lead a workshop in her Performance Studies class at New York University. The workshop we envisioned together would take the project, and me, from poetry to performance, yet there was new territory for engagement, affect, and expression. This would end in a song she wrote from words I had written in Toronto, although she did not know these words were mine. Barbara's song inspires me still. "The Beauty of weirdoes. Your human hope."

7) **Go around the room at least once and hear from all participants.** You might start with prompts that connect to feelings or knowledge about fake news and social media. At Devil's Dyke, we opened with exercises that connected us to the physical space of the room and our bodies. We talked about the devices that constantly disorient and distract us from the present as well as

the virtual "audiences" that we hoped or feared might be watching — including the men we might want, or hate, or fear — reminding us that the patriarchy is alive and well a decade or so after we had imagined and created worlds outside its gaze. In Brighton, there were seven of us, all queer feminists, mostly in our 20s or 30s, primarily British and white, writers and digital citizens all. We discovered that we all share similar experiences of our bodies when we are on social media, something akin to being inmates in a vision-prison that we enter willingly and remain within during all waking hours, a place where we could be "visited" anytime but never seen right, a place where we could never live up to the expectations constantly pressing us from all sides, *always checking* and being checked. We need to better notice (ourselves).

> I never noticed the tinnitus in my
> ears
> Always checking
> Cohesion
> and fragments
> together
> IMAGES
> MIRROR IMAGES
> Always there to push me back as
> I push in equal measure.
>
> — Group poem written at the Fake News Poetry Workshop at Devil's Dyke on March 19, 2018, in loose response to #100hardtruths #70: Reconnect the space that advertising has interrupted, which refers to the billboard intervention "Visible Distance / Second Sight (Gene Autry Trail and Vista Chino) for Desert X," by Jennifer Bolande.

As we go around the room, if I am a co-facilitator, the workshops *push me back as / I push in equal measure,* working in a friendly and open fashion to make connections between people's experiences and feelings about fake news and some of the bigger ideas in which these are situated. The pushing back is more like an adding to; not a correction but an expansion.

8) **Spend time getting to know each other.** For this reason, I often begin with an exercise that I have refined across this process:

> I ask participants to state one truth about themselves and then also to identify two *technologies* that could be used or engaged to "verify" that truth. I'm quick to define technology to include *any tool that extends the self to others through place and time*. Sure, the internet and other digital devices, but also pencils, flesh, and books. People get it: they grasp the formative inter-relations between lived reality, bodies, and our many mechanical and digital devices.
>
> — Alexandra Juhasz, "Forget the Audience: Reflections on the Process of Producing '10 Tries: 100 Poems,'" September 9, 2018.

I attempt to connect participants' contributions to a building idea about how we all live with and use combinations of technologies as a complex verification (and falsification) machine. As we ruminate and share, we discover commonalities as well as differences. Even as we learn that our perspectives are relative, we strive to remain open and truth-focused. To be honest, this is often quite painful. To be true: it seems we might be helping each other by doing so.

> We need new psychotechnologies through which we may be able to reclaim our capacity to pay attention in ways that are not self-destructive. ... And when we preserve and pass on forms over short or long timescales, it must be in part because we believe that these forms are not just aesthetically interesting but also that they are good for us (which is not to say "wholesome"). They give us ways of caring for our embodied minds and, by extension, to social worlds in which these embodied minds move.
>
> —Kyle Booten, "Psychotechnologies of Care, Algorithms of Attention."

9) **Attend to and care for ourselves and each other,** particularly in relation to the ways we feel about the internet.

> How does reading this make you feel? What are your reactions? What other questions, concerns, or even fears does this raise for you? What is the relationship of the body to the establishment of "truths," and/or beliefs? What is the body's reactions to the potential of those concepts being disproved, undermined, or otherwise threatened? Can you identify any reactions in your body? If so, what?
>
> —Elae (Lynne DeSilva-Johnson), from workshop handout, "Cartographies of Erasure: Perception, Justice, and Ethics in the Unapologetic Hyperreal." Occidental College workshop, Los Angeles, CA, March 5, 2018.

10) **Give permission to tell our terrible stories about social media.** As diverse as we are, and as each workshop is, not one participant has ever reported exactly liking the internet or themselves on and within it. If nothing else, these workshops serve as something like internet consciousness-raising groups, where people are authorized by the process and each other to hear and air dirty digital secrets and begin to understand these as collective, infrastructural, and definitive.

> I have a terrible story about social media |
>   SPIT IT
>   OUT
> lying is easier on the internet
> Does your body panic?
>
> —Written at the Devil's Dyke workshop as a loose response to #100hardtruths #83: Focus attention on the real-world applications of #fakenews.

11) **Do some research.** Next, we spend some time looking at my #100hardtruths–#fakenews media literacy primer: there is a version online and also a paper companion available in the form of a magazine. You can also ask people to do this in advance, that is, come with a favorite #100hardtruths that they want to discuss. Why were they drawn to it? What ideas or processes does it open for them? Workshop attendees are asked to find and then share something from the primer that feels resonant to them: an image, a piece of writing, a poem, an image, one of the #100hardtruths. This is to remind us that there is much to find and learn outside of ourselves and on the internet. We can rely on other people's work (on the internet!) to nourish, encourage, inspire, and even change us.

> The conversations that ensued were by turns uncomfortable and informative: all together, sharing a room

> that we had not recently inhabited, everyone was prompted to consider how they come to know the "truth" of very local political upheavals and of something as starkly divided as a dispute between management and workers. What channels of communication are in place in our lives that give us information about a labor dispute that is happening at our places of study, work, and living (the campus is all of these things in different ways)? What did people know from being on the picket line, or from official university communications, or from social media, or from conversations with other students?
>
> — Sam Solomon, "Truth and Lies at the Intersection of Activism and Art."

12) **Let the poet step in.** The poet has planned ways to discuss and actualize with the group the relations between creativity, writing, metaphor, truth, reality, fiction, and daily living. Having listened to and participated in the conversation thus far, she might ask a question or suggest a prompt for a free write. Perhaps she helps us return to the noise of our bodies, or to clarify and perhaps temporarily quiet that racket of the internet through our metaphors (please do see specific workshop plans online, they are collected under the ephemera of each distinct workshop). Our discussion, research, and feeling move to doing: art; poetry; performance; video. Our creative actions are framed by structures (our conversation, our experiences, the primer, the poet's prompt) that corral and link our thoughts and reflections.

> We opened with a free write asking participants to investigate when they first learned about race generally and then their own race. Specifically, we asked to
>
> - recall the first time you learned about race. How old were you? Where were you? What did you hear/learn? Draw into senses such as taste, smell, touch, color to describe; remember the first time you remember when you learned of your race;
>
> - recall the first time you saw your racial group represented in the media. What was this representation? Where were you? What do you remember? Describe beginning with I see...
>
> — Chet'la Sebree and Margaret Rhee, "10 Tries, 100 Poems (Take 8): 'Race in the Media — A Poetry Workshop,'" September 4, 2018.

13) **Ask questions about truth and about art.**

> The participants selected texts and images and separated them from their everyday contexts and functions, writing them into the poems. In so doing, they practiced abstraction — a practice which, following the logic of Evidentiary Realism, serves as a means of understanding the limitation of one's own vision of reality.
>
> — Orr Menirom, "10 Tries, 100 Poems (Take 6): 'Fake News, Video Poetry, and Evidentiary Realism @ Digital EngAGEment,'" August 2, 2018.

14) **Make some art.** During some sessions people write poems, or maybe only a fragment of writing, alone or together. At others we make videos or a performance. Sometimes participants

are invited to write a poem afterward, which they may or may not do. Participants are allowed to buy in at every step. Do it or don't; share as you are comfortable; things can go online or just go away. For the Devil's Dyke workshop, we wrote onto slips of paper our fleeting thoughts about our conversation and the many feelings it raised about and in our bodies. We laid those slips down on the floor in clusters, willy-nilly. We read these scatterings out loud. I recorded the proceedings on my smartphone. These different bundles of writing, performance, sharing, and meaning came together to powerfully and truthfully represent what we had been saying to each other, what we had heard, and what had been felt in the room; sadly, honestly, and with clear focus. But this was nothing like a one-to-one record, nothing like a photo; rather, our poems cut to loss, to want, and to the immaterial. Our poems were a pedagogic process.

> *Why poetry?* one faculty member had asked initially, after listening to Alex propose the project at an early meeting, bristling a bit (or so I thought) at its privileging. To me teaching means making something together in a room is always situational, sometimes also situationist. I said that I interpreted the exercise broadly as a chance to have a conversation with students about their experiences of language and art-making and their personal and political truths; to hear about their writing and reading practices; and to invite them to make work that related somehow to their socially mediated lives. I imagined that thinking about poetry with them would mean offering ways both open and constrained that they might use to respond in class and later to the issues Alex was raising.
>
> —Lisa Cohen, "10 Tries, 100 Poems (Take 7): 'Poetry and Pedagogy, A Beginning and a Continuation,'" August 30, 2018.

15) **Debate the truth.**

> The impulse of the project is to shift platforms from digital news circulation and refusal and rebuttal to poetic forms as a way to explore truths and lies. What is fake? This is the question that I think most grabbed our group: it seems none, or very few, of us were willing to give over to the binary of fake/truth but shared an understanding that these ways of shaping the world are themselves up for grabs; and aren't truth claims dangerous, the bedrock of colonialism and imperial occupation, and the justification for injustice? Indeed what is justice, even? We seek it, we talk about it together, at every turn we cultivate our understandings, learn new ways that justice escapes us, that we do harm.
>
> —T.L. Cowan, "10 Tries, 100 Poems (Take 5): 'Willful Healing Through Collaborative Collage,'" May 20, 2018.

16) **Make use of alternative formats for expressing ideas, answers, and more questions.** At some of the workshops, participants created a script and then performed it as a play.

> *Concept and Goals for the Play*
>
> - Creative methods (like performance, scripting, metaphors, images) are other useful formats to express,

explain, feel, and understand complicated analyses, difficult questions, and concepts with more than one answer; we want the play to manifest or contribute to the ideas above.

- It can visualize findings of research in an embodied and affective way in space and time and can be received as such.

- It is a powerful form to undo and redo logics that drive information disorder, recharging affective charges that have been used to manipulate users.

— Ioana B. Jucan and Alexandra Juhasz, handout for two linked workshops: HASTAC and Digital Methods Summer School, Vancouver, BC, Canada, May 18, 2019 and Amsterdam, Netherlands, July 1–5, 2019.

17) **Stay in the moment, in the place, and with these people.** We are moved and inspired, at least in the moment. We choose not to tweet or hashtag about it or each other. We find that a wider audience isn't needed. Or, better said, we have become each other's momentary witness and muse, and that seems more than enough. It feels empowering to forget the audience or acknowledge a more true if temporary one. We can create art that encompasses some of our experiences and thoughts, things we build together there and then about fake news and social media. These are truths we feel we could never discover or share solely online.

In the spring of 2019, I worked with Cathy James during several workshops held with her performance and writing group, Poets of Course. Some of the poems written by this group were later used as scripts for performances that were videotaped through a process of Cathy's design. I brought my longtime collaborator, Juanita Mohammed Sczapanski to shoot; later, Matthew Hittle edited them into video-poems. At these workshops, performers each embodied a word or line from a poem and then made a living sculpture from their gestures. We then produced soundscapes with our voices to render the moods of the poem with expressions outside of words. Cathy's Augusto Boalian techniques (the Brazilian founder of Theater of the Oppressed) — each person creating and refining a gesture that represented words from the poems or our conversations about them, and then producing sounds as a group — kept the art-making present in the room and our bodies.

18) **Share a purpose. Fall in love. Have a mixer!** Fake News Poetry workshops are hard-to-do, much-to-enjoy one-offs. I spend hours in advance working with a co-teacher to create a curriculum; we decide on methods to engage and stimulate our intimate group; I fly or ride somewhere and try to turn on my energy, as do my collaborators and participants. We are charged with purpose; we fall in love; we make art. The poems remain. We all go home. Does anyone read our poems? Does that "audience" matter in any way? Not really. We share what we have made with the others there with us as our primary witness.

Part 1: (now through 12:30) Start a conversation about media literacy, machine learning, and care. Lunch (12:30–1:00). Part 2: (1:00–2:00) Training a not-very-smart bot to take an ideological perspective. Part 3: (2:00–3:00) Performance + Time for everyone to discuss their own projects. Mixer (5:00)!

—Kyle Booten and Orr Menirom, workshop plan for Dartmouth College workshop, "Algorithms as Pets and Politicians," Feb. 25, 2019.

19) **Try and fail to display our vulnerability.** The radical digital media literacy is an effort to use technologies, including ourselves, to see and be seen, hear and be heard, know and be known, think and make sense, tell our stories, share our vulnerabilities, and fail so that we need to try again. I've seen it work—and believe in what it can do. It is my sense from the Fake News Poetry Workshops, and from the poems that record them, that we are in real need of new and old ways and places and formats and excuses to engage outside the sick and endangering structures and vernaculars that are born from corporate media ownership and the nations, citizens, or computers that abuse them to fuel the internet falsity under critique, principles like "growth by any means necessary." So, the project will stay as small and intimate and vulnerable as any of us can manage. We will do this, together; some things will get known and passed on; others will never be recorded or shared.

20) **Dare to be anti-solutionist.** Fake News Poetry Workshops work. In the doing they feel like a humane, ethical, and thoughtful response to the crisis of fake news. People come together. They think and make art. They listen and pass things on. They learn and show things about the internet and themselves. They take time to care. All this—so much!—is temporary, ephemeral, and small. It must be. Fake News Poetry Workshops will not end or undo the internet's current shape, or violence, or logics. Rather, they are process oriented: pro-being, pro-doing, pro-time, pro-art, pro-togetherness, pro-care.

Figs. 2 & 3. Cards that share affective responses to a deception: a prompt and response from the workshop held at the ArtEZ Workshop in Arnhem, the Netherlands.

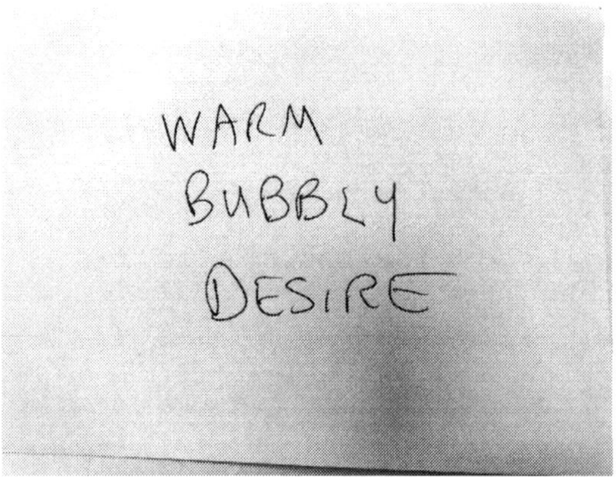

Fig. 4. ArtEZ affect card about a bodily response to deception. Penned by Alexandra Juhasz, prompt by Ioana Jucan.

We honor what is true about you, which will always be an open-ended process. How are we honest about this place? By doing so.

> How do you prove things?
> How do you create or feel trust, warmth, belief?
> How do you verify the truth?
> How do sounds, images, and words prove things?
> What is true about you?
> How can you be honest about this place?
>
> —Alexandra Juhasz, handout for New Utrecht High workshop, May 7, 2019. "Making a Fake-News Poetry Media Bank."

21) **Heed the poet's call**: a time-honored word-based form of truth-telling outside the logics of indexical mediation might be one well-honed literacy practice well-suited to this crisis.

Afterword
"... I sit with you": The Poetry, Media Praxis, and Worldbuilding of Alexandra Juhasz

Margaret Rhee

> "It is difficult / to get the news from poems / yet men die miserably every day / for lack / of what is found there."
>
> —William Carlos Williams

> "I don't cite you, I sit with you."
>
> —Participant in Toronto workshop

The dynamic pages of *My Phone Lies To Me* embody the multi-dimensional approaches of feminist media scholar, activist, and artist Alexandra (Alex) Juhasz's media and poetic praxis. Whether this praxis is illustrated in the form of Juhasz's pioneering work as a scholar and producer of documentary film, Black lesbian experimental cinema, HIV/AIDS activism, and educator in digital platforms such as YouTube, she has provided a model not only for praxis but for community as learning and building.

Juhasz's engagement with poetry is similar. This innovative book reflects the twenty-plus Fake News Poetry Workshops led by her and collaborating poets. Comprised of media theory, short essays, media praxis descriptions, workshop prompts, photographs, and most crucially poetry, this book reorients the reader to the intersection of poetry and media through Juhasz's political and creative approach to both. In the regime of "fake news," she demonstrates the power of citizenship and participation. As poet William Carlos Williams writes above in the poem "Asphodel, That Greeny Flower," poetry can hold the news, however in these times, perhaps the intersection of news and poetry is desperately needed. Juhasz's workshops and the corresponding book fulfills this gap and reveals the rich intersection of news and poetry through feminist praxis.

I'm compelled by the images in the book, and specifically the one in particular: "I don't cite you, I sit with you," written in bold Sharpie marker, and with the edges of perforated notebook paper. This phrase may be a "truth" written by a participant in a poetry workshop in Toronto. Makeshift, DIY, and community based, the photograph offers a small snapshot of how the workshops feels, and how Juhasz creates space. Here, individuals come together as communities. Instead of a hierarchical organization of space, she invites individuals and communities to "sit with her," "not cite." This approach embodies the possibilities of what she terms as "media praxis," a "wholistic linking of media production theory, and history with state goals of self- and world-changing," and it also reveals what poetry can do in light of media theory. A dedication to social justice or poetry intervenes in what we typically understand is the media scholar's domain, however she embraces both within this project and provides a new approach to the real and the fake news. As a subversive intellectual, she not only writes, makes, and teaches, but does what Fred Moten and Stefano Harney have written in their essay, "The University and the Undercommons: Seven Theses," steal from the university to create community-based space. Juhasz's radicality and positioning runs through the fabric of this project, in particular through a feminist "media literacy" infused with poetry and community.

The project itself started small, organically, and prompted by the need for change. Instigated by the November 2016 elections, Juhasz devoted herself to a personal project in which she would blog once a day about fake news for the administration's first 100 days. Through countering the fakeness of right-wing media, she found the public blogging as a means to help create a sense of order in a world that has and continues to disentangle. In this way, she finds a way out, and a method of redemption as she translates the "lies"' into possibility through digital blogging, documenting, and *heeding the poet's call.*

Perhaps we should go back to the beginning. By turning to poetry as a means of discussion and prompts, the Fake New Poetry Workshops are collaborations with poets all over the world that formed organic spaces with Juhasz. In doing so, she world builds a space where people do not stare at the screens of their lying phones, and instead, look at one another, speak with one another, and yes, sit with one another. This is the world I want to live in. In the book, she writes how poetry is "truth telling outside the logics of indexical mediation," and in the same way, her vision of the workshop setting, the translation of blogging political insights into poetics, does this work of the "truth": #100hardtruths–#fakenews. Through twenty-plus small and local workshops with poets and everyday people, *My Phone Lies To Me* is the manifestation of the intervention of feminist media theory and praxis with poetry. It reflects her vision grounded in grassroots organizing, and how the simple act of coming together lends itself to interventions to dismantle a Trump binaristic world.

I was there and I want to remember. Perhaps I'm also drawn to the images of the book as much as the poetry and short essays of media theory because I want to remember. With Alex's invitation of collaboration, my friend poet Chet'la Sebree, and I worked with Alex's project first at Brooklyn College in the Race and Media Workshop we conceptualized, then at a second time at Claudia Rankine and John Lucas's home where participants from other workshops joined us. In this workshop, we also collectively created poetic videos led by Alex and John in an innovative video and poetry workshop.

We sat together there. We listened. We wrote. We spoke. We created. I remember the faces, what people shared. And how we sat together and did not cite. In a time where those who identified as queer, immigrant, people of color, women felt constantly under siege, Alex gently led us in conversation, creating space together in a poet's beautiful home in New Haven.

This book encapsulates the radical manifestations of that day as much as language, image, and book can hold.

I'll end with a personal note. I first met Alex several years ago as a mentor in scholarship in feminist AIDS media theory where she has left an indelible mark supporting the collective feminist work I was doing in the San Francisco County Jail with her generous digital exchange. Alex's first monograph, *AIDS TV,* was a model for me and others, and when I met her in person, I found she was equally as generous and dynamic. More recently, members of my collaborating team who worked in the jail were invited to participate in the *AIDS, Video, Activism* screening at the LGBT Center Alex curated with *What Would a HIV Doula Do.* While my collaborators from San Francisco, Allyse Grey and Isela Ford, never met Alex prior, they were welcomed with Alex's characteristic open generosity and a demonstration of her feminist politics.

This book is like that encounter. It provides the rigorous thinking and generosity to organize people who are different to sit together, to think, write, and make. Poetry can be subversive, and the intersection of poetry and media can embody the kind of worldbuilding we need.

"I don't cite you, I sit with you." This phrase describes how Alex provides more than a theoretical intervention. Fake News poetry workshops and the pages of this book illustrates how we can confront a hardlined, dichotomous world into one that we can build and sit together, seeing the edges of the page as what it is: the start of remaking things anew.

Participants and Supporters of the Fake News Poetry Workshops

Ammerman Center. Sixteenth Biennial Symposium on Arts & Technology, New London, CT. February 15, 2018. Led by poet, technologist, and scholar, Kyle Booten, and attended by eight artists, archivists, and scholars.

ArtEZ University of the Arts. Arnhem, Netherlands. October 17, 2019. Participants included graduate students in Theater Practices with the support of their professors Pavlos Kountouriotis and Nishant Shah and with performance instructions created by Ioana Jucan.

Brooklyn College. Documentary Across the Disciplines class (DOC@BC). Brooklyn, NY. February 22, 2019. Participants in a class session building on three weeks of previous teaching by Joseph Entin (English), Jessica Siegel (Journalism), and Naomi Schiller (Anthropology).

Dartmouth College. Digital Humanities and Social Engagement Center. February 25, 2019. "Algorithms as Pets and Politicians," with Dartmouth students, professors, and staff, and the support of Jacque Wernimont. Led by Orr Menirom and Kyle Booten.

And a linked workshop at **International Studio & Curatorial Program.** Brooklyn, NY. May 20, 2019. Participants were studio members. Led by Orr Menirom and Kyle Booten.

Devil's Dyke Network. Brighton, England. March 19, 2018. Members, Linda Paoli, Claudia Treacher, and Helen Dixon devised and facilitated a workshop with six others in this queer feminist writing collective. My travels to England were supported by a Tow Research Grant awarded by Brooklyn College, City University of New York.

DIGITAL engAGEment: Media. Literate. #activist Conference. Held in Manhattan, NY. May 18, 2018. Conference hosted by Television, Radio & Emerging Media department, Brooklyn College. Workshop led by video artist, Orr Menirom, and attended by conference participants.

Emerson College. The Engagement Lab, Boston, MA. November 25, 2019. A workshop called Disinformation and Performance. Participants included students from co-facilitator Dr. Ioana Jucan's class, "In the News: The Real, the Fake, and the Spectacle," and graduate students and professors from Civic Media, Art, and Practice.

Feminist Poetics, Emergent Pedagogies Symposium. Los Angeles, CA. May 2018. Elae [Lynne DeSilva-Johnson] led an intimate workshop at the Occidental College Center for Digital Media Arts called Cartographies of Erasure.

HASTAC: Humanities, Arts, Science, and Technology Alliance and Collaboratory Conference. Vancouver, British Columbia. May 18, 2019.

And a linked workshop at the **Digital Methods Summer School.** Amsterdam, the Netherlands. The week of July 1, 2019. Both workshops were led by the performance scholar and artist, Dr. Ioana Jucan, in collaboration with digital theorist and artist, Roopa Vasudevan. Our many participants were international conference and summer school attendees. This research was undertaken, in part, thanks to funding from the Canada 150 Research Chairs Program, Dr. Wendy Chun, and the Tow Research Travel Fellowship from Brooklyn College.

Get Lit. Los Angeles, CA. March 3, 2018. A workshop led by Kelly Grace Thomas with fifteen teen poets.

And a linked workshop at **Get Lit.** Los Angeles, CA. October 13, 2018. A video-poetry workshop — led by Marcus James and Hanna Harris — where we (re)visited three poems written at the previous session. The videos were edited by Danny Nguyen. This was a collaborative effort with Occidental College's Center for Digital Liberal Arts. Their support enabled students and staff — Ash Tessier, Xiomara Rodriguez, and Aneesah Ettress — to document our process with a range of media.

Home of T.L. Cowan. Toronto, CA. March 17, 2018. A "a salon of co-creation," making the most of scholar and artist T.L.'s "cabaret methods" was attended by media artists, activists, and scholars, some local, many in town from around the world for the Annual Society for Cinema and Media Studies conference.

LaGuardia Community College. Queens, NY. April 24–26, 2018. Led by Lisa Cohen and engaging with scores of students in a poetry workshop, a literary club meeting, and an English 101 class, with support from professors and librarians, Tuli Chatterji, Ian McDermott, Lucy McNair, Chris Schmidt, and Ann Matsuuchi, with support from a grant from *Poets & Writers*.

New Utrecht High School. Brooklyn, NY. May 7 and 9, 2019. Student participants from an after-school arts program run by the Brooklyn College Community Partnership. Teachers, Rachel Garbus and Jeremy Goren, and Brooklyn College intern, Robert Rabin, worked with the students. Matthew Hittle edited their footage into poetry-videos.

New York University. Performative Writing class. April 10, 2019. Undergraduate students in the Performance Studies Department. Co-facilitated by Barbara Browning.

Occidental College's Center for Digital Media Arts. Poetry performance and media installation. Los Angeles, CA. March 5, 2018. Under the helm of Chris Gilman and with technical support from Craig Dietrich. These project supporters contributed time, space, digital resources, and staff assistance by Ash Tessier, Xiomara Rodriguez, and Aneesah Ettress.

Poets of Course. Manhattan, NY. October 2, 2018 and Spring 2019. Led by Cathy James working with fifteen or more disabled poets in a theater and performance group, with video assistance by Juanita Mohammed Szczepanski and video editing by Matthew Hittle.

Race in the Media. Brooklyn, NY. May 5, 2018. Led by Chet'la Sebree and Margaret Rhee working with ten or so primarily queer poets of color. Supported by a grant from Poets & Writers.

And a linked workshop at the **Home of Claudia Rankine and John Lucas.** New Haven, CT. November 3, 2018. This video-poetry workshop revisited poems from the previous workshop, with returning and new participants, as led by Orr Menirom, Kyle Booten, Chet'la Sebree, and Margaret Rhee. Video editing by John Lucas.

University of Buffalo. Buffalo, NY. March 10, 2020. Interactive Digital Humanities Event. Presentation of *My Phone Lies to Me* with workshop. Collaboratively sponsored in the College of Arts and Sciences by The Humanities Institute Digital Humanities Research Workshop, the Digital Scholarship Studio and Network, the Poetics Program, and the Department of Media Study with help from Drs. Cris Miller and Margaret Rhee.

University of Groningen. Groningen, Netherlands. December 7, 2020. "Fake News Poetry Post-Trump" with faculty and students in Arts, Culture, and Media Studies, with assistance from Dr. Annelies van Noortwijk. The project's only online workshop.

University of Sussex. Falmer, England. March 19 and 20, 2018. Experimental Writing class. Students led by their teacher, Sam Soloman.

Project Iterations: Participants & Supporters

Online Primer on Digital Media Literacy. #100hardtruths–#fakenews. Designed by Craig Dietrich and Xiomara Liana Rodriguez.
https://scalar.usc.edu/nehvectors/100hardtruths-fakenews/index.

#100hardtruths authored by invited contributors. Eve Oishi, Petra Kuppers, Geert Lovink, Theodore (ted) Kerr, Stephen Winter, Natalie Bookchin, Anne Balsamo, Kathleen Fitzpatrick, Cheryl Dunye, Jacqueline Wernimont, Quito Zeigler, Sam Feder, Nicholas Mirzoeff, Jay Fisher, Eileen Clancy, Gabrielle Foreman, Hugh Ryan, Laura Wexler, Faye Ginsburg, Antonia Juhasz, and Danielle Jackson.
https://scalar.usc.edu/nehvectors/100hardtruths-fakenews/26-100hardtruths-authored-by-contributors.

Scalar. Multi-modal authoring tool. The Alliance for Networking Visual Culture: https://scalar.me/anvc.

Paper Version of the Digital Primer. Designed by Craig Dietrich.
https://www.blurb.com/bookstore/invited/7501615/fe8b8c470c3e9c8d2e45267dddd62c85af9ebc1b.

Fake News Poetry project website and repository. Designed and built by Partner&Partners.
http://fakenews-poetry.org/.

Video-poems. By participants from Poets of Course, Get Lit, New Utrecht High School, Race in the Media, Digital Methods Summer School, Brooklyn College, Dartmouth College, and New York University. Edited by Matthew Hittle, John Lucas, and Danny Nguyen.
http://fakenews-poetry.org/media/new.html.

Podcast. *We Need Gentle Truths for Now.* With technical, artistic, and editing assistance from Julia Gill, Matthew Hittle, and Gavin McCormick. Featuring the voices of Chet'la Sebree and Margaret Rhee; Hugh Ryan, Simone Dunye, Frances Montenegro, and Eavan Anderson and the poems of Adrienne Rich, David Wojnarowicz, and Audre Lorde; Jih-Fei Cheng and Nishant Shahani and the poetry of Ross Gay; Alexandra Hidalgo; Sam Soloman and poetry by James, Shamine, and Marcela; Jason De León and a poem by Mike G.; Gabrielle Foreman and poetry by her father, Kent Foreman; the words and sounds of Claudia Rankine and John Lucas; the poetry and songs of Mika Judge and Joan Baez; Stacie Evans and Laura Wexler; Gerard G. and his mother, Vanessa Grant; Geert Lovink and Jacqueline Wernimont; Juanita and Henry Sczepanski; Natalie Bookchin and M. Astley; Frances Negron-Muntaner, featuring poetry by "Tato" Livaiera; Orr Menirom and Julia Gill; Dr. John Michael Cooper with the words and music of W.E.B. DuBois and Margaret Bonds; the music of Barbara Browning.
https://shows.acast.com/we-need-gentle-truths-for-now.

Book. *Really Fake,* with Ganaele Langlois and Nishant Shah (University of Minnesota Press, 2021).

Free PDF. *Really Fake* (meson press, 2021)
https://meson.press/books/reallyfake/.

10 Tries, 100 Poems :: Alexandra Juhasz :: Field Notes :: Fake News Poetry Workshops as Radical Digital Media Literacy (Series Introduction, edited by Adrian Silbernagle). Published by the Operating System & Liminal Lab. With writing about Fake News Poetry Workshops by: Kyle Booten, Kelly Grace Thomas, Anessah Ettress and Xiomara Rodriguez, Samuel Solomon, TL Cowan, Orr Menirom, Lisa Cohen, Chet'la Sebree, Margaret Rhee, and Alexandra Juhasz.
https://medium.com/the-operating-system/10-tries-100-poems-alexandra-juhasz-field-notes-fake-news-poetry-workshops-as-radical-ee2408808403

Other writing about the project. With the support of editors at *DAME, Radical Teacher, Preservation, Digital Technology & Culture,* and *Urgent Possibilities: Writing on Feminist Poetics and Emergent Pedagogies.*
http://fakenews-poetry.org/writing/new.html.

Funding. Much of my travel, and the small honoraria that I was able to provide for some contributing poets, editors, and technologists was supported by research and travel funds, as well as several Tow Fellowships, from Brooklyn College, with additional support from a grant from Poets & Writers. Poetry readings of this book have received support from a grant and fellowship from Social Practice CUNY.

As is clear from this long list of Participants & Supporters, this sprawling project touched many hands and lives, and asked for a great deal of almost entirely voluntary participation. What may not be clear is that this mostly unfunded project also had little administrative support beyond the labor of dedicated student interns and other folks who helped with many particular iterations of the project. I served as the project's producer: maintaining lists, generating permissions, linking places and people across space, time, media, and platforms. I end with this both to mark how DIY projects actually get done, but more so to say that any person who wasn't properly thanked, who wasn't named correctly, who fell off these pages is entirely a fault of my own barebones systems, but not an indication of very real appreciation and deeply felt thanks.

Printed in Poland
by Amazon Fulfillment
Poland Sp. z o.o., Wrocław

27433574R00083